T0209143

One Breath Away!

The Gospel of Peace

Treva Scott Thompson

WESTBOW
PRESS®
A DIVISION OF THOMAS NELSON
& ZONDERVAN

WestBow Press books may be ordered through booksellers or by contacting:

WestBow Press
A Division of Thomas Nelson & Zondervan
1663 Liberty Drive
Bloomington, IN 47403
www.westbowpress.com
1 (866) 928-1240

All Scripture quotations are taken from the King James Version.

ISBN: 978-1-9736-9331-4 (sc)
ISBN: 978-1-9736-9332-1 (hc)
ISBN: 978-1-9736-9330-7 (e)

Library of Congress Control Number: 2020910195

Print information available on the last page.

WestBow Press rev. date: 06/05/2020

To my daughter, Joni Lynn Soale, who has been very supportive, patient, and helpful during the writing of this book; and to my son, Brent Eugene Soale, and his family.

CONTENTS

INTRODUCTION

Condemn you? Oh! No, not I. I come that you might have life. I've been waiting, wanting to help you, but upward you did not look for no one let you know what was written in My book. The book of life—Oh! what a shame—never was opened to mention My name. I now come from the ends of the earth to tell you Myself of My humble birth. I walked each step that you have taken. Carried your load to keep you from breaking. Caught you when you were down and out. Remembered your name though the millions were about. Have you seen me somewhere? In a blooming rose? Or a mother's care? I've been all around you, just a breath away. Now that you have found me, this is your day. Rejoice! Forever, together we stay.

I did not know what this poem meant when I wrote it.

It has been life awakening.

These writings have let me voice what God showed me while bringing me out of darkness, and therefore, becoming truth to my soul.

I have attended church ever since I was born. Heard preacher after preacher; none knew or spoke of God's love. Oh! They read the Word with their thinking—fear, doubt, and unbelief—and preached condemnation. Do this, and do that, and God would love me.

Sadly, they had never met the Master. They would have known of His wondrous grace.

I searched the scriptures, knowing there had to be more than what

I had heard in the past. I sought God, and His words brought life to my wandering soul.

God showed me through His scriptures, His truth—line upon line, and precept upon precept—until I believed in a living God. He led me by His Word; nothing else.

I truly thank God for His mercy that He has for His children. He will truly not forsake us.

1

In the Beginning

(John 1:1-4) "In the beginning was the word, and the word was with God, and the word was God. The same was in the beginning with God.
All things were made by Him; and without Him was not any thing made that was made. In Him was life; and the life was the light of men."

Our life hinges on His Word. The Word is everything. The Word is God. The Word is trustworthy.
Traditions, rites, and rituals were the greatest challenges I had to overcome. My mind was full of the commandments of humans. These all pulled against the grace of God. The grace of God did not say, "Do this and do that, and then I will love you."

I found His love was free to all. Fear not! Only believe.

I have done a lot of searching in God's Word to clear the path for His love to rescue me. His Word is a lifeline that is always there.

The centurion asked Jesus to "speak the word only and my servant shall be healed." (Matt. 8:8). Jesus spoke the Word, and his servant lived. Jesus spoke the Word always—"Fear not, little flock; for it is your Father's good pleasure to give you the kingdom." (Luke 12:32). Believe His Word. He came to show us that we are children of God.

Jesus is the true light that lights every person who comes into the world. We are made in the image of God.

God is a spirit, and we are spirits. The first breath we take is receiving God's spirit. The light within us is that spirit. Fear takes over and keeps us from believing we are His children. We are made in the image of God. When that light is out, we cease to live on this earth. We are children of our heavenly Father. Jesus came as a witness to that. We are all children as Jesus, who is a child. Jesus gave His life to redeem us in the eyes of our heavenly Father. He washed away our unbelief. Jesus came to show us what it is like to be a child of God.

Fear not! Only believe!

The Word is the seed within us. It must be nourished to grow to maturity. It is not enough to only believe the seed is in us, but it needs to be nourished to grow. We must believe that He is the rewarder of those who diligently seek Him for we will find life abundantly.

Without the speaking of the word nothing is accomplished.

When the Word is declared, something happens. The life is in the Word. When we hear the Word spoken in our hearts and minds, life springs forth.

Our fleshly minds speak words that are not by the spirit of God.

We all have a fleshly mind and a spiritual mind within this natural body. They war against each other until the fleshly mind is renewed by the spirit of God that dwells within us. "And be not conformed to this world: but be ye transformed by the renewing of your mind, that ye may prove what is that good and acceptable, and perfect, will of God." (Romans 12:2).

Vanity is truly bondage for vanity is a spirit of this world. God does not give us the spirit of this world: fear, doubt, unbelief, failure, and falling. We are to be delivered out of these thoughts into the glorious liberty of God: trust, faith, confidence, love, understanding, peace, joy, and mercy. Romans 8:15–16 reads, "For ye have not received the spirit of bondage again to fear; but ye have received this spirit of adoption, whereby we cry, Abba, Father." Verse 16: "The spirit itself beareth witness with our spirit, that we are the children of God."

If we did not have fleshly minds, we would have been born believing we were children of God, as we were made in the image of God. Instead, our minds had fears and doubts about being children of God. God created humans to walk and talk with Him. Humans decided to not believe that God's love was enough. Their minds deceived them. They did not listen to the Creator.

For several days, the Word has been coming to me. (Rom. 8:31–32) "For if God be for us who can stand against us? He that spared not His own son, but delivered Him up for us, how shall He not with Him also freely give us all things." We are urged to come out of the spirit of this world. God did not purchase this world for us. He gave His Son to purchase life for us. Jesus paid that price, but we must be delivered out of bondage and corruption in our minds.

> "Who, being in the form of God, thought it not robbery to be equal with God: But made himself of no reputation, took upon him the form of a servant, and was made in the likeness of men." (Phil. 2:6–11)

The spirit that would cause us to draw back and not believe that we can think as God thinks is against God. Yet God says we are joint heirs with Christ. So, either we can let the mind of Christ be in us and know life, or we can let the mind of Lucifer sit in our temple and know death.

For human minds are death; they are transgressions against God.

> "But, if the spirit of Him that raised up Jesus from the dead dwell in you; He that raised up Christ from the dead shall also quicken your mortal [destined to die] bodies by His spirit that dwells in you." (Rom. 8:11)

This mortal must put on immortality. Our spirits shall not see death for God is life. This flesh shall perish and return to dust. But we shall be as the angels in heaven. We can dwell in peaceful places when we allow the mind of Christ to dwell in us. No unbelief can enter there; for if we have unbelief, we know from experience that we cannot grasp what God would have us believe. Peace has been opened to God's children. We can dwell there and have peace of mind. The wisdom God gives us comes through as clear as crystal. No unbelief can enter there.

We must believe that God is a just God before we are justified. Oh! How I praise God. It is a truth that sets us free. It is one more piece in the puzzle of the bondage I am in. Which comes right back to vanity. We can dwell in peace, and humans will not understand us if they don't know the power or goodness of our God. God is not willing for any to perish.

> "God is not slack concerning His promise, as some men count slackness; but is longsuffering to us-ward, not willing that any should perish, but that all should come to repentance." (2 Pet. 3:9)

God will deliver us if we diligently seek Him. To be meek is to be open-minded. To be humble is to put down every mind that comes against the mind of Christ for Christ's mind knew no limits. I have never heard it that way before, but it is spirit because it is bringing life to my mind.

The Word speaks about fasting the mind and spirit. Is that not the fast Jesus chose (Matthew 11:19)? They called Him a glutton, yet He fasted His mind and spirit. Therefore, He was able to do the works that the disciples could not do. I have fasted many times, thinking it would make God more apt to hear me. That was unbelief; that was not worshipping in spirit and truth. God does not want sacrifices and offerings. He wants a humble spirit and mind. Jesus chose to do His Father's will. His Father's will: was not His will until He chose it to be. He freely gave His life. No man took it from Him.

The willing and obedient can dwell in peace. To trust and obey— there is no other way. Jesus was not peculiar in His manner of dress. On the road to Emmaus, they knew Him not, for He was dressed like any other man. His kingdom comes without observation.

He said some would be standing here, which shall not taste of death, till they see the Son of man coming in His kingdom. (Matt. 9:1)

He is here in His kingdom today. Only those who look for Him will experience His visitation. Only lift Jesus up, and He will draw all people to Him. This spirit is brought out by the spirit of God. The blind men who called to Jesus could not see Jesus's form, but their spirits cried out, and then their eyes were opened. "And they which went before him rebuked him, that he should hold his peace: but he cried so much the more, Thou Son of David have mercy on me." (Luke 18:39). It is the same way with us today; our souls cry out until our eyes are opened.

Jesus "led captivity captive and gave gifts unto man." (Eph. 4:8). We are captive to the spirit of this world, or unbelief, until by His spirit we are captive to His mind. He came to make us free. He who the Son sets free is free indeed. It is every bit by faith. If we have faith, then we can believe and act upon that faith. Faith without works is dead. How do we act upon that faith? We not only believe it *can* be done; we believe it *will* be done.

I was at a prayer meeting several months ago, and a woman told the story of the mustard seed—the kind that was grown in Jesus's day. It would not grow or survive where there was anything else growing. It was pure and was easily choked out. Holy faith is pure. It will not survive alongside doubt and fear. When we have holy faith, the mountains will move. The Spirit will cleanse us from all filthiness of the flesh.

We need faith to move the mountains that loom over us. Jesus told the people, (Matt.9:29). "According to your faith be it unto you." Paul says in (Rom 12:2) "And be not conformed to this world: but be ye transformed by the renewing of your mind, that ye may prove what is that good and acceptable, and perfect, will of God." We have the mind of Christ, if, His spirit abides in us. If we have it, then we need it to be life to us.

God is so good to His children. His words are spirit and life. They do the work they were sent to do. The human mind shall not prevail over this nation.

God's people are a nation—a nation within a nation. Or hath God assayed go and take Him a nation from the midst of another nation? (Deut. 4:34). God has always had a holy seed upon this earth; many times, only a remnant was left, but it would enlarge and grow. Then sin would enter, and it would be cut off again, except for a remnant. When we obey the voice of our God, then we are free from the law of sin and death for humankind's way is death. It is no wonder God said, "The wayfaring men, though fools shall not err therein" (Isa. 35:8). The way of holiness. Complete trust. Not what we have always heard, not traditions, not Satan's oppressors, not Lucifer's mind, but listening to the voice of our God. He is to be King of kings and Lord of lords in our lives. How in the natural Jesus came as a baby; grew up in favor with God and humankind; conquered death, torment, and the grave; and then became King of kings.

How in the spiritual, when He first comes into our lives, we need to be nursed and fed by the Spirit. To grow up healthy and strong and come to full stature in Christ, and become victors over death, torment, and the grave, and then He becomes King of kings and Lord of lords in our lives. Unless God builds a house, they labor in vain that build it. If God does not help us, we will not be helped.

We are sure He will help us. I was thinking about Job yesterday, how God allowed Satan to afflict Job to show him His goodness. The devil meant it for evil, but God meant it for good—how great was the God Job was serving! Nothing is impossible with our God. There is no power but that which is ordained of God. God is still in the driver's seat.

"The glory of this latter house shall be greater than the former," saith the Lord of Host; and in this place will I give peace, saith the Lord of Host." (Hag. 2:9).

Sometimes, we forget there is no power except what is given by God.

2

My Peace I Send

"Peace I leave with you, my peace I give unto you; not as the world giveth, give I unto you. Let not your heart be troubled, neither let it be afraid." (John 14:27). Holy is the God of Abraham, Isaac, and Jacob. Holy is our God, and He has called us unto Himself. A holy people, an undefiled people, one whose God is the Lord.

Oh! The Holy Spirit impressed me: "His people are blinded; they are waiting to be raptured in the air." Jesus did not pray that. He said, "I pray not that thou shouldest take them out of this world, but that Thou shouldest keep them from evil" (John 17:15).

Jesus wanted us to follow God while we are here on Earth—He knew God's grace would keep us from evil—and leave the rest in God's hand to perform that which He would perform. He has overcome the world for us. "Hath raised us up together, and hath made us sit together in heavenly places in Christ Jesus" (Eph. 2:6). Only the truth will set us free. Why do we keep fooling ourselves by thinking we can interpret part of the scriptures right and part wrong? We cannot comprehend those things that are of the Spirit. I have heard preachers scare their congregations by saying that we must be careful, or else a wrong spirit will take hold of us.

That is wrong and contrary to God's Word. "Fear not, little flock it is your Father's good pleasure to give you the kingdom" (Luke 12:32).

If we ask for something good, He is not going to give us something evil. If the ministers could not set us free from that, why do we hold onto what we have been told about Jesus's second coming? I prayed earnestly that I might know what He was really like, and He has shown me. For months, I believed it was a wrong spirit, as it conformed not to my mind. Oh! The mercy God showed me until I believed. For it is exactly what Jesus preached, but they did not know the King of glory is the reason they crucified Him.

How His heart must ache when He brings the truth to us repeatedly, but we don't search, until we believe it. Jesus said, "For with stammering lips and another tongue will He speak to His people" (Isa. 28:11).

"Howbeit when He, the spirit of Truth, is come, He will guide you into all truth: for He shall not speak of himself; but whatsoever He shall hear, that shall He speak: and He will shew you things to come" (John 16:13). Yet we draw back from the truth He leads us into.

Lucifer sits right there telling us that God is leading us wrong. He says, "I will ascend above the heights of the clouds; I will be like the Most High" (Isa. 14:14). God has never led anyone wrong. People are led wrong when they refuse the truth. We are all not only to believe what comes out of our mouths. "Out of your belly shall flow rivers of living waters" (John 7:38). We are to believe our minds to be the mind of Christ when our minds are transformed, when we are sold out to God, and when we realize Satan is a liar and there is no truth in him. The son of perdition never did anything good but instead causes us to draw back from the truth, which is ready to set us free.

We are not to think that Christ's mind is going to deceive us. We are God's people. We are not to fear but have complete trust. Lucifer is fallen; his hold is loosening. Fear shall not have dominion over us. Jesus was manifested to destroy the works of Satan.

His second coming is by the Spirit. God's people don't have to perish for lack of knowledge. He says, "Ask and it shall be given you; seek and ye shall find; knock, and it shall be opened unto you:" (Matt. 7:7). God's church is at the threshold of the mind of Christ.

Is not Lucifer doubling up on all sides to prevent that? He knows our rightful place with God, although we have been blinded to it, but the Word says our blinded eyes are going to be opened: "To open their eyes, and to turn them from darjkness to light, and from the power of Satan unto God, that they may receive forgiveness of sins, and inheritance among them which" are sanctified by faith that is in me." (Acts 26:18).

I had felt what it was like to have wisdom without charity. It was very empty. Then I began to read: 1 Corinthians 13:1. It had to be possible to have all these things and still not know what it was like to know Jesus. His words overcome the beast, and the image of His testimony became very real. I began to read in Revelation 13:4 "They worshipped the dragon which gave power unto the beast: and they worshipped the beast, saying: Who is like unto the beast? Who is able to make war with him?" So the beast had great power. Jesus had warned His disciples that false Christs would come, and if it were possible, they would deceive the very elect. Stop! Think how real that is. Looks real, sounds real, uses the scriptures, but it just does not taste good. The fruit is not ripe. It is bitter and hard to digest and does not bring life to our souls. It fails when put to the test. That is what my other book, *The Fruit That Is Ripe Is Always Sweeter*, is about.

These ministers pray in the name of Jesus but sound like they don't even know of God's grace. Are they blaspheming His name, as in Matthew11:12: "The Kingdom of heaven suffers violence, and the violent take it by force"? Could it be that the beast is hiding under the name of Jesus? There is no name that is higher or can receive honor higher than the name of Jesus. Now I began to see how the people were being deceived. The people were looking at the miracles and not the source from which they were proceeding. This is a covering that is not of God.

Their power is from some other source: "For we wrestle not against flesh and blood, but against principalities, against powers, against the rulers of darkness of this world, against spiritual wickedness in high places." (Eph. 6:12). He is revealed for what he is, an accuser of the brethren. Any kingdom divided against itself cannot stand. The beast casting out the beast comes to naught when the strongman of the house binds him and then spoils his goods. We are not to fear him; we are to reverence God.

Narrow is the way, and few there be who find it. God is merciful to some by pulling them out of the fire "and others save by fire" (Jude 1:21–23). God has sheep scattered without shepherds, but they are hearing the voice of the good Shepherd and another voice they will not follow. For they know His voice.

We need to pray for those God gave to Jesus, that not one would be lost, nor overlook the least or the greatest, that none of their precious blood will be on our hands. Now I began to see how different it is to go forth showing the love that God has for His children compared with what the beast shows: condemnation, holier-than-thou attitude, oppression, depression, and fear. God lifts with His arms of love, whispers peace and takes away oppression, heals the brokenhearted, and sets the captives free. The son of perdition is being revealed. The King of glory is stepping out on the scene, and who shall stand the fire? Only those to whom the Father hath revealed Himself shall overcome the beast and his image.

Jesus said, "Not everyone that saith unto me, Lord, Lord, shall enter into the Kingdom of heaven; but he that doeth the will of my Father, which is in heaven" (Matt. 7:21).

They were workers of iniquity, though they had gifts and miracles. The gifts and miracles and their tongues were not of God. God is holy, and He does not uphold sinful people.

3

Greetings in the Name of the Lord

Greetings in the name of the Lord Jesus, the Lord of heaven and earth. Oh! I praise God for His goodness to humankind. He is not a man that He should lie. What He has said He will do. He still speaks today, so we know for certain that He is still performing His Word.

"Let this mind be in you which was also in Christ Jesus" (Phil. 2:5). We all need a mature mind, the mind that was in Christ. We need patience. We have the living God dwelling within us. What more could we hope to have? The creator of heaven and earth, the maker of all living things. He has not turned a deaf ear to our needs. He still stands beckoning us to listen to His voice and have complete trust. There is no way possible to have peace of mind until we humble ourselves to listen and wait upon the Lord. How big is this God we are serving? Did He let Daniel be eaten by the lions? Did He let the three Hebrew children perish in the fire?

Did He let Jesus die in vain? No! He has never done us any harm. It is not in His plan to do us harm. He redeems His own every time they need redeeming. We don't have to repent day in and day out, God is there; instantly, God is there. He is constantly working for our good. This is not something to be lived on church night and Sunday; this is life itself. Nothing good will He withhold from us. We know there is no other way of life for us. We are not our own. I know they call us dreamers and say we are living in a fairyland, but it is real, and it works.

Fear and torment and worry don't deliver anyone, but faith in a living God does. We need to have patience, wait on Him to lead us, and not get impatient as a child would.

God's people are a needy people. The need is to listen to His voice. God delivers His people, and if we are depending on God to deliver us, then we must determine to listen to His voice so we can be delivered. Fear will cause us to just halfway listen to what God says. Maybe He is right, and maybe not. That is partaking of the tree of the knowledge of good and evil. God is right; not us. God, we are going to wait on You.

I find it hard to keep from limiting God by trying to fit Him into the plan we have always known. If we are going to dwell in peace, then we are going to say, "Lord, lead me and guide me every day." People may say we are out on a limb, but while we are there, His Word is going to hold us in our minds, for where He leads us, He will feed us.

The more His Word shakes our minds, the more we will know what truth is, shaking out all the old thinking. If we are new creatures, then we should have completely new thinking. I mean thinking that delivers, not thinking that binds. New wine in new bottles.

God is leading us into a more excellent way. The love that God has for us is the kind of love God wants us to have for one another. He wants the God in us to minister to the needs of one another. "For, he that eateth and drinketh unworthily eateth and drinketh damnation to himself, not discerning the Lord's body. For this cause, many are weak and sickly among you and many sleep" (1 Cor. 11:29–30).

It is not in the miracles. I believe it is in the love of God—a love that is greater than all our unbelief, fear, and doubt; a love that cares, a love that understands, a love that God is opening to me, that I had never known. I don't feel guilty for not knowing this. If I had been ready for anything, God would have opened it up to me sooner. God is leading us step-by-step so we can stand and not just run the race but keep the faith and finish the course.

The work He wants done can be done right and not have to be redone. We should wait both patiently and quietly for the salvation of our God. Now those words are as true as the rest that are spoken. We can't ignore His word and go God's way at the same time. God's army never lost a battle. "Blessed is the nation whose God is the Lord, and the people whom He hath chosen for His own inheritance" (Ps. 33:12). He now has that people and is going to redeem us back to our Creator. Back into the image of our God. We must decrease so God can increase.

I began to wonder just what the scripture says concerning how to live in the Spirit. "But the fruit of the Spirit is "love, joy, peace, long-suffering, gentleness, goodness, faith, meekness, temperance; against such, there is no law" (Gal. 5:22–23).

There is a place He would have us occupy, and we will occupy if we listen to His voice. If we do not listen to His voice, then we are partaking of the devil's table, and the devil never offers anything but torment.

4

God's Mercy

God's mercy is from everlasting to everlasting unto those that fear Him. I realized there is sorrow in the minds of humans: "For godly sorrow worketh repentence to salvation not to be repented of: but the sorrow of the world worketh death." (2 Cor. 7:10). God did not bring the truth to me for myself alone; He brought it as a deliverance for all His people. "If the Son therefore shall make you free, ye shall be free indeed" (John 8:36). As we lay down our lives for our friends, we forsake our own ambitions and desires in life and set our faces, determined to bring truth to everyone around us.

If what He shows me does not agree with my thinking, I pray until God gives me light. We have never been this way before; so that lets me know we had better have open minds, or transformed minds, or we will not be able to follow for long.

God has been teaching me about holy health: how what we think upon has a lot to do with our health. Torment and worry can cause ulcers. Bitterness and hatred can cause our bodies to throw off a poison to disrupt bodily functions. Fear can grip our whole being. "Be not wise in thine eyes: fear the Lord and depart from evil. It shall be health to thy navel and marrow to thy bones" (Prov. 3:7–8). Faith, trust, and love can create healing for they are life. These other things are death.

It made me understand more clearly. When I pray for people, I usually pray for their minds first. I couldn't understand why, and at times, I was embarrassed. (Most people don't want to think there is anything wrong with their thinking.)

He is bringing us out by His Word. "Let this mind be in you, which was also in Christ Jesus: Who, being in the form of God, thought it not robbery to be equal with God:" (2 Phil.2:5-6). If we live, there will be wars, sickness, death, and sorrow in this world.

God paid the price that we may have peace of mind, be raised up above that, and still have our feet on this earth. Heaven holds! If God be for us, who can stand against us? We have determined to do the Father's will, so a way will be made where seemingly there is no way.

5

A God of Judgment

Praise God for a God of judgment; Who judges us by His love and by His mercy.

I awaken this morning to the verse, "He treads the winepress of the fierceness and wrath of Almighty God" (Rev. 19:15). The thought came to me, *Do I believe those things enough to declare them?* I began to draw back. I've had to use this scripture over and over the last few days: "For God has not given us the spirit of fear; but of power, and of love, and of a sound mind" (2 Tim. 1:7).

I began to search. There is no power but that which is ordained of God. Why is there a devil who could have the spirit of fear to come against us? I went back to the garden of Eden, the tree of life, and the tree of the knowledge of good and evil. There I stood partaking of the tree of the knowledge of good and evil. I believed, but I had unbelief. I had faith, but I was afraid. I knew what was right, but I was afraid. I could not trust my mind. God said if Adam and Eve partook of that tree, they would surely die. "But of the tree of the knowledge of good and evil, thou shall not eat of it: for in the day that thou eateth thereof thou shalt surely die." (Gen. 2:17).

Unbelief is not going any further for unbelief cannot enter. Complete trust was my answer. Whatsoever is not of faith is sin. I then read, "They were both naked, the man and his wife, and were not ashamed" (Gen. 2:25). We must be naked concerning our own minds. We must not be ashamed to declare we know nothing except what God tells us. God disclosed to Adam and Eve that He had given them everything that they would ever need.

The serpent said, "Ye shall not surely die" (Gen. 3:4). He intimated that God had not given them all; he implied that God was leading them wrong. "Let this mind be in you, which was also in Christ Jesus: who being in the form of God, thought it not robbery to be equal with God" (Phil. 2:5–6).

God wanted some fruit from His labors. The Word was setting before me the tree of life and the tree of the knowledge of good and evil. You hear people say children are at the age of accountability when they know right from wrong. Spiritually, I was at that place. I am a babe in Christ.

By being immersed in the love of God, it is truly overwhelming to think of His mercy to me. When I would ask God to open the Word to me, He always did. When I asked him to fight my battles, He never failed. I was double minded. I see I've always had to declare it before it became salvation unto me. It was the truth inside of me, but my mind is not God's. It was declaring the truth that set me free.

"To do justly, to love mercy, and to walk humbly with our God" (Mic. 6:8). God had given all to help me have complete trust in Him. Oh, I'm glad for Zion, for therein is deliverance. I now see the tree of life in the New Jerusalem for the healing of the nations. He has healed my mind. I can't help but cry. No one could have been as blind as I was. Yet step-by-step, He led me out of the awful depth. Now we have power over all power of the enemy. That power does not bring rejoicing. God's love and mercy to me are all I can think of. He has given me a right to the tree a life.

Several nights ago, I went to pray. I kept repeating the scripture, "Behold I will send my messenger, and he shall prepare the way before me: and the Lord, whom you seek, shall suddenly come to his temple, even the messenger of the covenant, whom ye delight in: behold he shall come, saith the lord of host." (Mal. 3:1). Then it seemed as though I wrestled most of the night.

God just now gave me that portion of the song by Henry Francis Lyte: "Change and decay in all around I see, Oh! Thou who changes not abide with me."

I thank God for His goodness to humankind.

6

God Is So Wonderful

God is so wonderful; all He has ever wanted was for us to listen to His voice and obey. By listening to His voice and trusting, we are obeying. When we are not listening to His voice, fear creeps in and we give form and life to that fear. We cannot form God for He is life.

I find out more and more that God is in each person. He just needs to be awakened and brought forth. The real transgressions against God are fear, doubt, and unbelief. So many of His people are in so much darkness, which obscures the truth. We fear and doubt that God is in us. That is the Antichrist. Love, which is trust, is greater than anything else.

Isn't God a good God? A God of love, mercy, gentleness, meekness, kindness, and long-suffering will go to any length to redeem us back to our Creator. He knows just what we need and goes ahead and gives it to us before we realize we need it.

It sure is wonderful to have Him dwell within us, because the spirit is willing to follow God and will cry out, "Not my will, but thy will be done." I found the same words in Luke 22:42. It is the Word that gets the work done; when we don't see how it could possibly be done. I'm learning that God's Word is still His Word, whether it comes from the Bible or by the unction of the Holy Spirit.

His Word is not going to fail. It is quick, powerful, and sharper than any two-edged sword, piercing even to the dividing asunder of soul and spirit. I've never seen that before, but now I can clearly see. The soul is the life God breathes within each person. His Word will cut loose any spirit that would cause our souls to have unbelief for His Word is truly life.

Two weeks in a row, my pastor told about Jesus folding the napkins and laying them aside. He was not in a hurry while He was in the tomb. As the pastor finished telling that story, I remembered a scripture. I looked it up this morning. "Therefore, thus saith the Lord God, behold, I lay in Zion for a foundation a stone, a tried stone, a precious corner stone, a sure foundation: he that believeth shall not make haste" (Isa. 28:16). "For ye shall not go out with haste, nor go by flight: for the Lord will go before you; and the God of Israel will be your rereward" (Isa. 52:12). Every act Jesus performed was just fulfilling some prophecy. In quietness and confidence shall be your strength. We truly have a loving Savior.

I can't recall the many times He washed my eyes with tears that I might see. Before church last night, as I was praying, I was reminded that He was going to open blind eyes and put love in the hearts and minds of His people. I must be one of His people, for His love flooded my soul. He has shown me how love and mercy are going to "wash away the filth of the daughters of Zion" (Isa. 4:4) for it is His goodness that brings us to repentance. It is love that we can't resist or gainsay. I can see more and more that it is about the love of God, not by condemnation.

The pastor told us all to believe in the resurrection. So, it had to be something more than what we were believing. The scripture reads, "We know that we have passed from death unto life because we love the brethren. He that loves not his brother abides in death" (1 John 3:14). Jesus laid down his life so that we might have life. He put aside hurt feelings, pride, lust, and greed, and He paid the debt that each one of us owes.

We are indebted to one another to love one another. We owe that to each other. No one lives or dies to oneself. I can see how love heals the wounds of others. His Spirit revealed to me by His Word a long time ago that charity is the love God has for His children. I can see why He told us to "walk in love" (Eph. 5:2). For God's love for us will never fail us; it is a faithful love. It is pure undefiled, sweet, and kind.

I used to cry out, "God, you said to love our enemies" (Matt. 5:44). I knew I wanted that kind of love. I knew there had to be a greater love, for God has showed forth that greater love toward me. "My little children let us not love in word, neither in tongue; but in deed and in truth" (1 John 3:18). We can say we love if it doesn't involve us. If truly, we love it will show. The most blessed part of it all is that unless we get this love from God, we shall never get it any other way.

It is no wonder Satan goes about as a roaring lion seeking whom he may devour. He has known what God's love is like and knows he will never have a part in God's love again. Satan was cast out of heaven and has nothing more to lose.

7

Learning to Love

If we have never learned to love, we have never truly lived. We will not partake of life until we know death to self. I realized the other day that one of the keys to the kingdom is to cast out fear, and hate will go. We fear something, or we would wait. We may fear we will miss out on something or that someone will not accept us.

I began to search out that scripture that reads: There is no fear in love; but perfect love cast out fear: because fear hath torment. He that feareth is not made perfect in love." (John 4:18). If we have perfect love, then fear can be cast out, and there will be no hate. Love covers a multitude of sins, and if they are covered, we won't be able to see them. If we don't see them, what is there to hate? If we have complete trust in God, then there will be no fear. Death hath no more dominion over us when we know God's love in our lives.

I can see how Paul could glory in his infirmities for they were exactly what Paul needed to keep him following God. Paul prayed three times that God would remove that thorn in his flesh, but God told him: "My grace is sufficient for thee: for my strength is made perfect in weakness." (2 Cor. 12:9). I can look back and see the very thing I asked God to remove was the very thing I needed to learn what God would have me learn. He would have us learn love. He allows something, or someone, to linger until we either submit to or reject

His love. If we reject His love, then we will have lived in vain. He is that long-suffering and a big enough God for every situation.

I wish I had learned a long time ago what I know now, but I would not understand how others feel had I not suffered as they. Experience, with God as the leader, is still the best teacher. Everything else will fail us but God's Word. His Word assures us that charity will never fail. I failed to see how anything could help us. He says He is not only the author but also the finisher of our faith. God never starts something good and then drop it off. He knows where He is going because He has been there. John knew that Jesus was the son of God: when the dove set on His shoulder. When there is love, then there is peace in life. I am guilty of not reading the Word for myself but just listening to what was preached. I knew not at the time that I was doing that. Just because I believed something did not make it right.

The spirit has cried within me all along, *God, if your will is not done, I will never be happy.* So He keeps leading me on, and the road keeps getting sweeter each day.

I have always loved this: "Now is come salvation, and strength, and the kingdom of our God, and the power of His Christ" (Rev. 12:10). He dwells within His people to comfort us. "Thy rod and thy staff they comfort me" (Ps. 23:4). To give us true comfort, He wants to speak to His people, but because of their fear; They refuse to listen. It is His Word that is life, and if the Word is spoken, it will come to pass.

He would that we all prophesied that we all might learn. Prophecy is the testimony of Jesus, and we can gain victory over the beast when Jesus speaks. We don't realize, His Spirit, that is within us can bring us back to fellowship with God—back into the garden, back to walking and talking with our heavenly Father.

8

The Light of God's Word

The waters shall no more become a flood to destroy
all flesh.

—Genesis 9:15

People turning their backs on God are causing their own deaths for the
wages of sin is death. But there are a few that are riding on the waters,
and God has remembered them as He remembered Noah. After the
rains had ceased and the waters abated, He gave them dominion
again upon the earth. After Lucifer has been cast out of our minds,
then peace can come in. We have been returned to the Bishop and
Shepherd of our souls. The Word reads that we are to "be fruitful, and
multiply, and replenish the earth," (Gen. 1:28). We can bear children,
spiritual children who believe in God and choose to serve Him. We
want to serve Him willingly. For the willing and obedient will eat the
good of the land. He must be Lord and Master of our lives.
We will be long-suffering as He was with us. We were not spoiled,
but with His great love and mercy, He chastened us. He fed us butter
and honey, as Jesus was fed (Isa. 7:15), "that He may know to refuse
the evil and choose the good." We are not to spoil others but tell
them the truth. We are trees of righteousness, planted by the rivers

of living water. We will build on the solid rock, Christ Jesus, because whatsoever is born of God overcomes the world.

"Vengeance is mine, I will repay, saith the Lord" (Rom. 12:19). "The wicked shall be turned into hell, and all the nations that forget God" (Ps. 9:17). The man of perdition is being revealed; he is being cast out. God said this would not come except there be a falling away. "For the time will come when they will not endure sound doctrine; but after their own lust shall they heap to themselves teachers, having itching ears; and they shall turn away their ears from the truth, and shall be turned unto fables" (2 Tim. 4:3–4).

God's people need to be taught to listen to the Holy Spirit's voice. He speaks. They cannot distinguish His voice. I believe His people have two minds: carnal and spiritual. The devil is very bold at stealing away the Holy Spirit's words. For His words are comforting and bring peace of mind; they are gentle and not condemning. The devil's words are very condemning and leave you beat down, depressed, oppressed, and ready to give up.

When God chastens us, He refuses to leave us there; He shows us the way out to higher ground. Why do we think that we can think our way out? The only way Jesus defeated the devil was by the Word. He was rooted and grounded in the Word. It is the power of God unto salvation.

That makes me think of a time at prayer meeting; I left my Bible at this woman's house. It was as if I had left my best friend. I went the next day and got it. I remember holding it very tightly and crying, and I remembered the scripture: "It is the power of God unto salvation to everyone that believeth;" (Rom. 1:16). I was a believer, but I was in gross darkness from the truth. Oh, God has been so merciful to me. I can truthfully say He is a long-suffering God, more ready to give than we are to receive. God loves His people. He is true to His people Israel. "Neither will I hide my face anymore from them: for I have poured out my spirit upon the house of Israel, saith the Lord God" (Ezek. 39:29).

I have heard people say there has been enough gospel preached to save the whole world. I have a very odd feeling when I hear them say that, for I was practically born in church. After I believed, I wrote a poem. "The Book of Life had never been opened to mention His name." (I mentioned that at the beginning of this book.) I did not know the meaning at the time when my spirit gave me those words, but they were comforting; they burned inside of me. I remember after believing, the day that I found out Jesus loved me— plain ole me, just the way I was. I remember crying and thanking God for His mercy. God had caused me to bury myself in His Word, and He did come Himself in His Word to show me the truth.

The second coming of Jesus is opening to me altogether differently than how I have ever heard of it. I still do not understand it all. It has taken three years or more. It will be four years since I believed. I must have patience and follow just as close as I can. I have a desire to speak only what God would have me speak. Not some new idea, just the truth, but really the truth is new, for Jesus is here in the flesh, in a temple not made by hands. It is new to God's people. They are groping away off somewhere to a God who, maybe, if they are good enough, He will hear them. "My people are destroyed for the lack of knowledge" (Hosea 4:6). "His visage was so marred more than any man" (Isa. 52:14). I thought that meant that they had put thorns on His head and nails in His hands and feet and pierced His side. That was not it at all. When Jesus came in person He was not recognized. They knew not who He was. Today, as He comes in the Spirit, they know not Him. A person can be set up in a kingdom on this earth. Everyone knows about it. They know not the King of kings. His kingdom is within humankind. It is not with observation. "He shall not cry, nor lift up, nor cause His voice to be heard in the street" (Isa. 42:2). I could not understand that. Did not Jesus preach and rebuke the scribes and Pharisees in the temple? Was He not heard? Then He gave me the scriptures in the New Testament where He made Himself no reputation. "Why calleth me good? There is none good but one, that is, God" (Mark 10:18).

The Word reads, "Go ye out to meet Him" (Matt. 25:6). Now the Word reads, "Surely I come quickly. Amen. Even so, come, Lord

Jesus." (Rev. 22:20). That took me back to Isaiah 62:6: "I have set watchmen on the walls, Oh! Jerusalem, who shall never hold their peace day or night." Then I read of Ezekiel's wheel in a wheel: "And they everyone went straightforward: where the spirit was to go, they went; and they turned not where they went" (Ezek. 1:12).

Could that be God's redeemed being spoken about in Revelation 14:4: "These are they which follow the Lamb whither so ever He goes" I do not understand it all; for the Holy City of Jerusalem is real to me. The Bible reads that "Babylon the great is fallen, is fallen, and has become the habitation of devils and a hold of every foul spirit, and the cage of every unclean and hateful bird" (Rev. 18:2).

Did not Noah enter the ark with his family before it started to rain? At that time, they probably did not see the need of going into the ark before it started to rain. But when it started to rain, God shut the door. And the people probably didn't even realize the door was shut until judgment began to be poured out, and then it was too late. Just as with the ten virgins and their lamps … Five were foolish and they had no oil. In other words, His words were not written upon the heart and mind; their light was not burning.

If we do not have the light of His Word dwelling within us, we will not know the day of His visitation until judgment begins to fall. Then every eye shall behold Him. I pray that I might find the truth and not draw back, for it is easier to retrieve than it is to listen to the "still small voice" and go forward. Abraham moved when God said move. He just obeyed and pulled up stakes and moved: "and strengthen thy stakes" (Isa. 54:2). There is a children's Christmas song, "Toy Soldiers on Parade." My spirit will sing that through me when there is a battle raging. God's army is marching to victory. And they have on their royal garments also.

Jesus died and rose again. "He that findeth his life shall lose it: and he who loseth his life for me shall find it" (Matt. 10:39). He lost His life, but by losing His life, He found life—life everlasting. When He was resurrected, He had a glorified body. Nothing had any hold on Him now. He went to be forever with the Lord.

When we crucify the flesh and the lust thereof, then we walk, and we live in the Spirit. The Word reads, "This mortal shall have put on immortality" (1 Cor. 15:53–54). "But if the spirit of him that raised up Jesus from the dead dwell in you, he that raised up Christ from the dead shall also quicken your mortal bodies by His spirit that dwelleth in you" (Rom. 8:11). Jesus was crucified, went into the grave, and was resurrected; and Christ arose.

I've never seen this before; it is all spiritual. Repent, be born again. Repent from not believing we are God's children (made in His image). Whosoever is of God sinned not and kept himself from the evil one. When we were born He breathed into us His spirit and we became a spirit.

Did not the disciples eat with Jesus after He was resurrected? He had a body, yet He was a spirit; for He could appear in a room with the doors shut. Can we not pray in our homes and have our words help someone miles away?

We are spirits. Spiritual death, torment, and the grave have no hold on us now. We shall forever be with the Lord. I believe this is the "rest" to enter: a natural being and a spiritual being.

Earlier I read: "As we have borne the image of the earthly, we shall bear the image of the heavenly" (1 Cor. 15:49). Now I know what it means. God is a spirit. If we are made in the image of God, we are spirits. We are God's children forever and forever. I see now how Jesus has the key to death, torment, and the grave. Jesus was crucified. Jesus crucified is the everlasting gospel.

> "That your faith should not stand in the wisdom of man, but in the power of God. Howbeit we speak wisdom among them that are perfect; yet not the wisdom of this world, nor the princes of this world, that come to naught: but we speak the wisdom of God in a mystery. Even the hidden wisdom, which God ordained before the world unto our glory: which none of the princes of this world knew for had they

known it they would not have crucified the Lord of Glory" (1 Cor. 5:9)

As it is written: "Eye hath not seen, nor ear heard, neither have entered the heart of man, the things which God hath prepared for them that love him" (1 Cor. 2:9). Right on down, that chapter sings of the love of God. We have two minds until Jesus is the head; then we go whithersoever the Lamb goes.

I hope I have written it down as clear as it appeared to me. "This is the will of Him that sent me, that everyone which sees the Son, and believeth on Him, may have everlasting life: and I will raise him up at the last day" (John 6:40). The last shall be first and the first last. If the gospel be hidden, it is hidden to those that are lost.

"Which in other ages was not made known unto the sons of men, as it is now revealed unto His Holy apostles and prophets by the spirit;" (Eph. 3:5). You are God's people, a holy people, for He is a holy God. Every promise in the book is ours. "For the earnest expectation of the creature waiteth for the manifestation of the sons of God" (Rom. 8:19). That chapter reads on down how the whole creation groans and travails in pain together until now. May God richly bless, as I know He will.

9

God Is Long-Suffering

God is long-suffering, so I must be patient.

Oh! The unsearchable riches God has kept until this time. He has kept the best wine until last. People pray that God's will be done; then when it is done, they refuse to see it as God's will.

"Blessed and holy is he that hath part in the first resurrection: on such the second death hath no power, but they shall be priests of God and of Christ, and shall reign with him a thousand years" (Rev. 20:6).

"Now therefore ye are no more strangers and foreigners, but fellow citizens with the saints, and of the household of God;" (Eph. 2:19). Our conversation is not of this world. The way I see it, in the beginning was God, which is spirit. The word was with God, and the word was God. In the beginning God created heaven and earth. There was spirit and earth, but there wasn't any form to the earth, so God took His spirit and put it in a body—"His legs of iron, his feet part of iron and part of clay. Thou saweth till that a stone was cut out without hands, which smote the image upon his feet that were of iron and clay and break them to pieces" (Dan. 2:33-34).

So, God took this spirit, putting it in clay, but clay weakened the spirit, so God sent His spirit back to make a perfect spirit again unto himself. I hope I'm making it clear. So, through Jesus we are a perfect spirit again. We are God's children. "But they which shall be accounted worthy to obtain that world, and the resurrection from the dead, neither marry, nor are given in marriage" (Luke 20:35). God said His Word was spirit, so it must be interpreted by the spirit. "For thy maker is thine husband; the Lord of hosts is His name; and thy redeemer the Holy one of Israel; the God of the whole Earth shall He be called" (Isa. 54:5).

We are His love, His church, His bride, His spirit returning to Him. "This I say, brethren, the time is short: it remaineth that both they that have wives be as though they had none" (1 Cor. 7:29). I see that if we are now living in the spirit, spiritual things come first. Then these other things will be added. We are spirits; we are to communicate with God. If we have been quickened, who were dead in trespasses and sins, that is the resurrection. The second death has no power over us. Stephen was a good example. The Word reads if we are not willing to forsake all and follow him, then we are not worthy of him. "This is a great mystery: but I speak concerning Christ and the church" (Eph. 5:32). Solomon in all his wisdom does not even halfway compare to the wisdom of God.

In that hour Jesus rejoiced in spirit, and said I thank thee, O Father, Lord of heaven and earth, that thou hast hid these things from the wise and the prudent, and hast revealed them unto babes: even so Father; for it seemed good in Thy sight. (Luke 10:21). Why babes? Because He said we were to become as little children. I see now more clearly than ever why God is not willing that any should perish. It shows why He is so long-suffering.

John fell to worship before the feet of the angel, who said, "See thou do it not for I am thy fellow servant, and of thy brethren the prophets, and of them which keep the sayings of this book: worship God." (Rev. 22:8–9). God does not share His glory.

10

Sorrow

For around three weeks I have been weighed down. Last Thursday night, I realized it was sorrow. I began to read the Word: "He is despised, and rejected of men, man of sorrows, and acquainted with grief" (Isa. 53:3). Many things have happened in the last three weeks. All I could seem to do was groan and cry when I prayed. I began to look back through some things I had written down; one was this: "You will meet the man in their minds." "Woe to that man by whom the Son of man is betrayed" (Mark 14:21).

I looked back through my writings: "Charity cannot fail; it does not know failure. Failure is not known. Failure cannot be uttered, for it cannot prevail against my church. For my church is a holy church."

I began to read the scripture: "A lowly Jesus, a lowly Nazarene, despised, forsaken unloved, and unclaimed." He is despised and rejected of men; a man of sorrows and acquainted with grief" (Isa. 53:3–5).

I had begun to read about Jesus being betrayed. "My soul is exceedingly sorrowful, even unto death: tarry ye here, and watch with me." (Matt. 26:38). For that cause came He unto this hour. Jesus had prayed until "not my will" was His answer (Luke 22:42). Jesus knew who was to betray Him, but He showed love all the way through for it was in God's plan.

The Word began to open-up Jude, so very clearly to me. Judas had walked with the twelve and had even leaned on His breast, yet he failed of the grace of God. "Have not I chosen you twelve, and one of you is a devil?" (John 6:70). The Word began to show me God's children and the devil's children. Judas had been with Jesus along side the other disciples. He had walked and dined and stayed with Jesus, but His spirit was not the same as the other disciples. He had not fully surrendered his life to following Jesus. He looked like one of the disciples and no one would know the difference. But when it came to defending Jesus, he was not there. His heart was not right.

Abel offered up the living unto God as an offering. Cain offered fruit of the earth, which was cursed. In the garden Adam and Eve did not till the ground; they took care of the living, which God had created. Abel offered God part of the living that God had given him. God still wants a living sacrifice today. He wants life, our lives; nothing short will suffice.

Our dead works will not be accepted. Cain could have turned from his way and went Abel's way. If he had done well, God would have still taken his gifts of life; but sin lay at the door. He thought his way was the right way. He thought he had offered the right offering, but when he found out he hadn't, he would not repent and turn. Instead, he slew the righteous one.

> "For the mystery of iniquity doth already work; only who now let's will let, until he be taken out of the way" (2 Thess. 2:7)

> "Little children it is the last times; and as we have heard that antichrist shall come, and even now are there many Antichrists; whereby we know that it is the last time. They went out from us, but they were

not of us; for if they had been of us, they would no doubt have continued with us: but they went out, that they might be made manisfest that they were not all of us. But ye have an unction from the Holy One, and ye know all things." (1 John 2:18)

(1 John 3:10-14) "In this the children of God are manifested, and the children of the devil: whosoever doeth not righteousness is not of God, neither he that loveth not love his brother."

"We know that we have passed from death unto life, because we love the brothen. He that loves not his brother abides in death; whosoever hated his brother is a murderer: and ye know that no murderer hath eternal life abiding in him."

"Do you think that Scripture saith, "In vain the spirit that dwells in us lusts to envy?" But He gives us more grace. Wherefore He saith, God resist the proud, but gives grace to the humble. Submit yourselves therefore to God, resist the devil and he will flee from you" (James 4:5-7).

"If my people, which are called by my name, shall humble themselves, and pray, and seek my face, and turn from their wicked ways; then will I hear from heaven, and will forgive their sin, and heal their land" (2 Chron. 7:14).

People, in their own minds, are evil continuously. They can only know death to spiritual things. God is not willing that any should perish, but Judas did. The son of perdition is here today, but the Son of man came unto His own, and His own received Him not.

It seemed the sorrow of knowing this was more than I could carry. "For Godly sorrow worketh repentance to salvation not to be repented of but the sorrow of the world worketh death" (2 Cor. 7:10). Mine had been the sorrow of this world. It worked death. The pride of life is not of the Father but is of the world. If we save our lives, we shall lose them.

This morning my spirit began to speak about "a holy rest for this day. You must lay down the sorrow; it is more than you can bear."

"He is a rewarder of those who diligently seek him" (Heb. 11:6), and He is "the beginning and the end, the first and the last," and "the author and finisher of our faith" (Rev. 22:13).

The book of Jude is clear to me now. "Therefore, it is no great thing if his ministers also be transformed as the ministers of righteousness, whose end shall be according to their works" (2 Cor. 11:15). Their works are iniquity (unrepented sins). My spirit spoke: "They will never admit they are wrong." If they don't admit they are wrong, how can they repent? I cried out, "Never, Lord, never?"

Only God can hold us when all has forsaken us. I remember many months ago I cried out, "My God! My God! Why hath thou forsaken me?" (Matt. 27:45–50). Christ arose triumphantly over death, torment, and the grave. A man child is born, not one in the manger, not still a baby.

A song by Jim Reeves has kept me through these days:

WHERE DO I GO FROM HERE.

> "Through the grace of God alone, I'll cast aside those fears I've known, and lift myself from the depths of deep despair. Oh, give me strength that I might find, abiding faith and peace of mind, and I won't ask where do I go from here."

Here's another song by Jim Reeves that comforted me:

OH ! GENTLE SHEPHERD

"While wolves are waiting for the night; to claim the soul that wondered from the fold. Oh! Gentle shepherd, hear my cry and lead me home."

It is night and the wolves have waited until now. But God's Word, which is spirit, will put them to flight.

11

A Lot to Learn

There is lots and lots to learn.

We once yielded our members to learn humankind's way; now we yield our members to learn God's way. The way is made so plain when only Jesus Christ crucified is preached by the spirit. I can see all the many souls that are drowning in themselves; because of their fear, doubts, and unbelief's are keeping them from believing Jesus paid it all. It is that simple. Jesus paid it all. Just receive!

By observing lying vanities, they forsake their own mercy. Last fall when I read about vanity in the Word, the word *bondage* seems to be the way it was described. "The creature was made subject to vanity, not willingly, but by reason by he who hath subjected the same in hope" (Rom. 8:20).

"All that is in the world, the lust of the flesh, and the lust of the eyes, and the pride of life, is not of the Father, but is of the world. And the world shall pass away, and the lust thereof: but he that doeth the will of God abides forever" (1 John 2:16–17).

We are subject to vanity but not willingly. (Eccles. 1:13-14). "This sore travail has God given to the sons of man to be exercised therewith. I have seen all the works that are done under the sun; and, behold, all is vanity and vexation of spirit."

He put Adam and Eve away from His presence to make a living on this earth by their own minds.

So therefore, we are subjected to our minds. We are in bondage to our own minds until God's spirit is within us to lead and guide us into all truth. Then we have a choice set before us, as Adam and Eve did, to partake of the tree of life and live, or partake of the tree of the knowledge of good and evil and know death. If we know to do right, then we can do right. We have a choice to listen to God or follow the imaginations of our own hearts and minds, which will separate us from our God. "Because the carnal mind is enmity against God: for it is not subject to the law of God, neither indeed can be" (Rom. 8:7). This world is a spirit that holds us to it.

We can rise above this world into the glorious liberty of the children of God. Vanity is bondage. All that people can think or do, "flesh and blood," cannot inherit the kingdom. "Be not wise in thine own eyes: fear the Lord and depart from evil" (Prov. 3:7).

We have only to glory in Christ Jesus. "Where is the wise? Where is the scribe? Where is the disputer of this world? Hath not God made foolish the wisdom of this world?" (1 Cor. 1:20). No flesh should glory in His presence.

We have not received the spirit of this world. Therefore, our minds cannot feed us, but we have received the spirit of God.

Wherefore the spirit knows the things that are freely given to us by God. There is no other foundation to build upon, save Jesus Christ for the wisdom of this world is foolishness with God.

He takes the wise in their own craftiness. The thoughts of the wise are vain. I fall back on Mary and Martha many times. Mary was not of this world. Martha was of this world. They both yielded their members to whom they were servants. Martha satisfied the lust of her mind. Mary sought peace of mind.

Jesus humbled Himself when He found Himself a man. He did not follow humankind's mind. He took upon Himself the form of a servant. A servant has humbled himself by not having a mind of his own. To please his master is his one aim in life. Then Jesus said, "Henceforth I call you not servants; for the servant knoweth not what his lord doth: but I have called you friends; for all things I have heard of my Father I have made known unto you" (John 15:15). Jesus was born not in the high and mighty place in His day; He was born in a humble manger.

Jesus is born today in a humble and contrite heart. The high and mighty, refuse to see Jesus. Oh, they talk about Him. They have strong willpower and think they are enough in themselves. (So did Adam and Eve; the end of them was death.) But their minds are going to fail them. One of these days, there is going to be a situation they cannot get out of by using their minds. Then and only then will they fall on their knees and acknowledge there is a mind higher than theirs. We are God's children, but there is only one God. We have a choice to listen to our own minds, but we know better than to do so.

When the spirit of this world is shaken; it doesn't remain. When the spirit of God is tried, it delivers; it remains for it is built on the solid rock Christ Jesus.

Whatsoever is of God overcomes the world. If it is of Jesus, it will stand. If it isn't of Jesus, it will fail at a time we need it most. If what we believe delivers us, then hold on to it. If we think for a moment it seems right but when it is tried it fails, then we are to cast it aside for it is not of God. God's words are life.

We are judging angels. God made angels ministering spirits. They come to minister unto us. God does not give us a spirit of fear but of love and power, and a sound mind. I realize more and more that the devil is a liar. The other day God's spirit set me free from a lying vanity, and before I realized it, I said out loud, "Devil, you are a liar," and I have said it several times since then. "For he is a liar and the father of it." (John 8:44).

A friend said his friends called him a hypocrite because he went to church and then to the bar. He told his family that God had healed him, but they refused to believe him. His wife said he told them it was true; whether they believed him or not, he had been healed. We need to be delivered from a lot of things in our lives. God understands and is long-suffering as we seek Him.

12

Mysteries

I am thankful for the mysteries of God that are being revealed unto me. When I started writing this book, I was hoping I would be able to convey what I had learned. With God as my helper, I shall try.

The tabernacles of God are with humankind. In Revelation the song to the Lamb, the Lion of the tribe of Judah, praises Him because He has "made us unto our God kings and priest: and we shall reign on the earth" (Rev. 5:10).

I know I am not as other people, and yet God said that we are "a peculiar people" (1 Pet. 2:9).

To me the joy of the Lord is my strength. The money we make and bring home to buy things is not our joy for it is God who gives us power to get wealth. The credit goes right back to God. Everything that is good comes from God. I believe the fruit of our lips should be praises unto our God, from whom all blessings flow.

The zeal God had placed within me was not of my doing, but I had the choice to serve God or humankind. But this earth cannot hold us; we are not of this world. In (Rom. 8:19) we read that "For the earnest expectation of the creature waited for the manifestation of the Sons of God." The passage goes on to note how the whole earth groans and travails in pain together until now.

If we are trying to find our way to a new place. We will need directions from someone who knows the way. We should accept the challenge that the Bible has for us. God says, "I counsel thee to buy of me gold tried in the fire, that thou mayest be rich; and white raiment, that thou mayest be clothed, and that the shame of thy nakedness do not appear; and anoint thine eyes with eye salve, that thou mayest see" (Rev. 3:18).

If He instructs us to ask, seek, and knock, then we must do those very things. "Ask and it shall be given you" (Luke 11:9). His Word is the only road map. There are no shortcuts or detours. Patience will win out, as God protects you from failing. I cannot find where He ever forsakes His children. He lifts them and carries them above the storms that are raging. If someone told you this was the road to New York, then you would have faith that this was the right road to travel. We must have it settled in our hearts. We must count the cost. "And whosoever shall not bear his cross and come after me cannot be my disciple" (Luke 14:26-27). The price is our lives—to live holy before Him and wholly for Him.

Our children must see that we love them even if they never measure up to what we think they should; that is in the natural. In the spiritual it is the same. God loved us when we refused to believe we were His children. What makes us love God is that He has showed forth such love for us. We must show forth love for our children. The truth will root up, pluck out, and cut down, but it must be proclaimed. It is the truth that will set us free. It may be hard sometimes and very painful; it may disgrace us in the eyes of others; but we must pick ourselves up and dust ourselves off, or we can never be used. So many will not do that.

Noah's children; couldn't see the need of entering the ark at the time that they entered, but it wasn't long until the rain began to fall. We can claim our household. "She is not afraid of the snow for her household: for all her household are clothed with scarlet" (Prov. 31:21). Parents are to guide the home.

13

Everything as It Should Be

I would like very much for everything to be as it should be here in our home first, but God knows best. Maybe I wouldn't seek God as I do if it were so. I thought of what the pastor said last night. "If he did what God had asked him to do, then all things would be taken care of." I bought a record several days ago, and I played one song over and over, hearing Longfellow's familiar words:

> "I heard the bells on Christmas Day, the old familiar
> carols play, and round and sweet the words repeat of
> peace on earth, goodwill to men. I thought how as
> the day had come. Etc."

As I listened to that record, I thought of the angels singing it. I believe the wrong shall fail and the right shall prevail. I believe we shall have peace. I know it will cover a multitude of our problems.

We are in this world, but we are not of this world. Jesus said, "I pray not that thou shouldest take them out of the world, but that thou shouldest keep them from the evil" (John 17:15). If we are not of this world, then our conversation is not of this world. Jesus had perfect fellowship with God while He was here on this earth. He and His Father were as one. He said, "No man hath ascended up to heaven but He that came down from heaven, even the Son of Man which is in heaven" (John 3:13). Jesus was here on Earth and said that He was in heaven. God said, "Heaven is my throne" (Acts 7:49). Is not that throne within humankind, the one the King sits upon?

The earth is His footstool. God dwells in earthen vessels that the excellency of the power may be of God. We are the new bottles to hold the new wine. This wine in old bottles would offend and break them. He says, "Behold, I create new heavens and a new earth: and the former shall not be remembered, nor come into mind" (Isa. 65:17). I've never heard of this before, but you know Paul knew from whence his message came, therefore he did not bow to please people. This has been a struggle, how unbelief and fear have played a part in my life.

When God's Word revealed to me that I was a child of light, then fear began to lose its hold. "Ye are all the children of light, and the children of the day: we are not of the night, nor of darkness" (1 Thess. 5:5). If you put a light in a dark room. That room isn't dark any longer. As that light grows brighter, all darkness is dispelled.

The truth has set me free again. God has chosen me. It was not my doing. God has led me step-by-step by His Word, not my mind, because my mind was always proven wrong. Jesus said, "Fear not, little flock; it is your Father's good pleasure to give you the kingdom" (Luke 12:32). Oh, the joy of serving a living God. I thank God for His goodness to the children of humankind.

I read, "He is the God of the living" (Mark 12:27). Also, "With long life will I satisfy him" (Ps. 91:16).

There is no limit to what God has for His children, if we walk in the light as He is in the light. "I thank thee, O Father, Lord of heaven and of earth, because you have hidden these things from the wise and prudent, and hath revealed them unto babes" (Matt. 11:25). There must be a spiritual meaning that the natural human knows nothing about. God says His words are spirit.

The Word reads, "But when that which is perfect is come, then that which is in part shall be done away" (1 Cor. 13:8–13). Nothing is hidden from God. He sees everything. When God sits on His throne, we see him and everything that passes our way. In anything that happens to us, God should still be praised.

I was undecided who to vote for. I prayed, and it was still not clear who to vote for. I remembered the scripture that says the government will be upon His shoulder (Isa. 9:6). That was Jesus's shoulder. Then I read in Romans 12:2, "Be not conformed to this world." Then I thought of what the Pastor had said about the soldiers: if they leaned on God's arm, they would come home. They were not only to lean on their natural resources, but upon God.

God is our God and we are His people. Also, we read, "That I have been young, and now am old; yet have I not seen the righteous forsaken nor His seed begging bread" (Ps. 37:25). We are to look to God, from whence cometh our help. We are not dependent upon the president. We are to look to the Lord. I believe God will help me vote for the right one. The president needs our prayers to help him have wisdom to deal every day with his performance as president.

God had chastened us that we may be partakers of His holiness. Without holiness we cannot see God in all things.

The hour that we quit our thinking, then Jesus comes to take His abode. "Watch therefore for you know not what hour your Lord doth come" (Matt. 24:42). I thought of Caleb this morning. One out of each tribe was chosen to search out the Promised Land. "Only Caleb had another spirit with him and have followed me fully, him will I bring into the land where into he went; and his seed shall possess it" (Num. 14:24). Caleb was of the tribe of Judah. Caleb knew his God. They would have rather stoned Joshua and Caleb than believe they could take the land. God stepped in.

The people had God in their midst up to the Promised Land, but they still could not see Him. "As truly as I live all the Earth shall be filled with the glory of the Lord" (Num. 14:21). Even though the world does not believe, that does not make God a liar. It just makes them unbelievers. His will shall be done.

14

Kingdoms Shall Rise and Fall

Down through the ages, kingdoms arise, and kingdoms fall.

> "So shall my word be that goeth forth out of my mouth: it shall not return unto me void, but it shall accomplish that which I please, and it shall prosper in the thing whereto I sent it" (Isa. 55:11).

The ministry of reconciliation is reconciling people back to God. There is a rest wherein He calls the weary to rest. We can pray in the spirit even at home and pull-down strongholds. Then when we meet others bound by those spirits that have been put under our feet, we can speak His words and bind those spirits and release God's people.

Jesus told Peter "I will give unto thee the keys to the kingdom of heaven: and whatsoever thou shalt bind on earth shall be bound in heaven: and whatsoever thou shalt loose on earth shall be loosed in heaven" (Matt. 16:19).

God ceased from His work and rested the seventh day. God would have us cease from our work and enter that rest. "This is the rest wherein ye may cause the weary to rest; and this is the refreshing: yet they would not hear" (Isa. 28:12).

Even as Jesus said, "I and My Father are one" (John 10:30). If they had known Jesus, they would have known the Father. We are not to think it robbery to believe God is our Father for we are a habitation of God, the tabernacle of God, the temple of the Holy Spirit—God the Father, God the Son, and God the Holy Spirit.

God's love always wins out. If God's people just knew how much He loved them, fear and torment would have to flee, for perfect love casts out fear.

During one of the services a lady came up in front to be prayed for. I looked at her, and she was looking at me, but she was very calm for a moment. I told her God knew her heart and that it was crying out to Him, and she nodded her head yes. I said it is our minds that keep us torn up, and she agreed. As I think about it, I could have been the one standing there in her place. I had trusted my soul with God. I had trusted my heart with Him; He never broke my heart. Why couldn't I entrust my entire mind to Him?

I had trusted the biggest part with Him, but a little leaven leavens the whole lump. That little bit that I was keeping back was keeping me from having liberty. It was keeping Him from sitting on His throne in my earthly temple. All the earth had not kept silent yet. God's Word reads, "Let all the earth keep silent" (Hab. 2:20), but not all had been put under my feet.

I have been called a liar more often in the last six months than I have been called by my right name, but the Word let me know God had put a fence (hedge) around me, It is truly there, because those things don't oppress me or discourage me. We must truly learn to love those who despitefully use us, and then we must turn right around and even feed our enemies when they are hungry.

I read in (Rom.11:28-31), "As concerning the gospel, they are enemies for your sakes: but as touching the election, they are indeed beloved for His Father's sake. For the gifts of God are without repentance. For as ye in times past have not believed God, (that was me.) Yet have now received mercy through their unbelief: even so have those also not believed that through your mercy, they also may obtain mercy."

We can pull them back out of the fire (Jude 1:21–23).

"Be thou faithful unto death, and I will give thee a crown of life." (Rev. 2:10). God is still in the driver's seat, and He is from everlasting to everlasting, so we must just walk each day at a time. As I prayed, these words came to me: "Mercy, go teach mercy." I began to dig into the Word. Jesus came to be the Savior of the world. If He came to be the Savior of the world, did He fail, or did He save the whole world? Back in Ezekiel 18:4: "Behold, all souls are mine; as the soul of the Father, also the soul of the son is mine: the soul that sinneth, it shall die." Jesus came to buy that soul back into fellowship with its Maker.

The pricks that Paul was kicking against was that still small voice of his soul crying out within him that there is a God. (Acts 9:5).

Paul had tried to quiet that voice. When he was struck blind, he knew who was talking to him. Jesus is not willing that any should perish. Jesus came to save the world from their sins—sins of not worshipping God and worshipping the creature instead of the Creator. Jesus did come, Jesus did take away the sin, and the wages of sin is death. He was taken from among the living because of our sins. Jesus paid that wage for us. Once was all that is needed, for it was a perfect sacrifice. People don't know that their soul is in bondage. The Word showed me that my soul and my mind were in bondage. "I am the Lord thy God which hath brought thee out of the land of Egypt, out of the house of bondage" (Exod. 20:2). I didn't feel worthy to praise God and believe that He loved me. My mind needed healing. Then when the truth is brought to us, that Jesus came and through Him all guilt and shame can be erased, then we can awaken unto life everlasting—or not believe and turn away and be damned.

It is not the carnal soul that is against God; it is the carnal mind. I believe that our minds are causing our souls to sin. My pastor has said that if the devil would leave the carnal person alone, he or she would find God. God's spirit was breathed into each soul when we were born. We believed not.

I was the only one that was up in our household, and I was fixing dinner for that day. The neighbor man was sitting on his porch. As

I looked over there, my spirit prompted me, and I said, "Your soul is saved." I believe he didn't realize he was saved.

Then I began to say, "Every soul is saved, because Jesus bought them back." Our minds separate us from God. Our minds will keep us busy doing everything but worshipping God. Elijah thought he was the only godly one left, but God let him know that there were many who knew there was a God and worshipped Him as such. Many church people have always had that holier-than-thou attitude. Remember! God saved the sins of the whole world.

Sin is death; the carnal mind is death; to follow our mind is death or sin. Fear, doubt, and unbelief are the sins of God's people. "But your iniquities have separated between you and your God, and and your sins have hidden His face from you, that He will not hear" (Isa. 59:2).

Eve sinned. She followed her own mind. God says, "Come out of her, my people, that ye be not partakers of her sins, and that ye receive not of her plagues" (Rev. 18:4–5). It is our minds. He said we must serve Him with all our heart, soul, mind, and strength, to be worthy of Him. We must forsake all for Him.

If every soul is saved, why does it say repent? Repent from the sin of following our minds, repent from not praising God from whom all blessings flow. Repent from our unbelief that God is in us. "Bless the Lord, O my soul, and forget not all His benefits" (Ps. 103:2). I believe millions are like the dry bones: can they live again? "Behold I shall cause breath to enter into you and ye shall live" (Ezek. 37:5). Through Jesus, anyone can live who believes.

The angel had told Peter to follow him out of prison, and if Peter hadn't believed to follow him, even though the gates were already open, Peter would still have been in prison if he had not believed and followed the angel out.

I wrote a poem right after I became a believer: "To tell a prisoner he is free, is indeed in vain: if he does not arise and unshackle the chains: Jesus died for you and me and we must believe it before we are free. Jesus came that we might have life, true peace of mind instead of strife. If you are striving for peace of mind, in Jesus Christ that peace you'll find."

Why did Moses want Pharaoh to let the people go? To worship God. Why did God harden Pharaoh's heart? So He could bring them out with signs, wonders, and miracles, "For the scripture saith unto Pharoah, Even for this same purpose have I raised thee up, that I might shew my power in thee, and that my name may be declared throughout all the earth" (Rom. 9:17). Why do we have trials and tests? "When he is tried, he shall receive the crown of life" (James 1:12). It is to show forth God's righteousness and not our own. The Word began to pour through me. Then Satan began his work in my mind, making me afraid to tell it in ways I had never heard it before.

All day I was tormented in my mind, afraid to tell what my spirit had showed me. The battle was the Lord's, and He won out that day. I felt I was being led to where no person had ever been.

I read the scripture, "How that by revelation he made known unto me the mystery" (Eph. 3:3–4). These things all help. His Word says we can have a holy mind. "Be ye Holy; for I am Holy" (1 Pet. 1:16). I reasoned that if I had a holy mind and my thoughts were holy, but all I ever heard in the churches was admonitions not to get in the flesh. But they never bothered to teach us how to get in the spirit; we were already in the flesh. We needed to learn of the spirit.

Most of all, I was fearful to prophesy, afraid it would be out of my mind or heart. I began to pray most earnestly to prophesy. It was a matter of life or death to my mind. I cried out, "Lord, to prophesy unto your people. I believe these other things will be added. If not, then all things work together for good to them that love the Lord and are called according to His purpose." The Word lets us know the price is high. "If any man will come after me, let him deny himself, and take up your cross, and follow me" (Matt. 16:24–25).

15

Wisdom of God

Oh, the matchless wisdom of our God. We are not the children of darkness anymore, for the Lamb is the light thereof.

I had been asked to read where it says about the man being the head of the woman, and for them to keep silent in the church.

It never really bothered me too much, as I always came back with the answer: If we were in the spirit. we were neither male nor female, but yesterday I was praying, and it all began to be revealed to me.

Man was made in the image of God. Adam called his helpmate woman. In Genesis 2:23, I read that woman was "taken out of man." Anything that comes from man should be kept silent in the church of the living God. When we come to full stature (man or woman) and are made in the image of God, then that which comes out of us will be as the oracles of God, not as something from us.

We have control as to what comes out of us, when we are brought back to complete fellowship or perfect fellowship with God. "I see that the head of every man is Christ; and the head of the woman is man; and the head of Christ is God" (1 Cor. 11:3). It goes on and tells about having our heads covered and uncovered. We should have our minds covered by the mind of Christ.

Our minds are the offspring of humankind. When we are born of God and have come to full stature, we become adults and put away childish things. Then we are thoroughly furnished unto all good works. That which was taken out of man was deceived (Eve). So male or female should keep silent in the church. Only the spirit should speak. It goes back to "The Lord is in His holy Temple; let all the earth keep silence before Him" (Hab. 2:20).

Judgment begins in the house of the Lord. Judgment begins in us. "Whose fan is in His hand, and He shall thoroughly purge His floor, and gather His wheat into the garner; but He will burn up the chaff with unquenchable fire" (Matt. 3:12). When the husband and the wife both have the mind of Christ, then they two become one. When we become as one in Christ, Christ in us, and we in Christ, and God the head, then God will add to his church daily. "For more are the children of the desolate than the children of the married wife, saith the Lord" (Isa. 54:1).

God's church is going to bear children, and the children are going to be different than the church that uses condemnation. What was so different about Solomon's kingdom? All the servants were happy and there was peace. "Happy are thy men, and happy are these thy servants, which stand continually before thee and hear wisdom." (2 Chron. 9:7). It is wonderful to serve a living God and not dumb idols.

A harlot isn't married. A bride is married. We are the bride of Christ. We shall bear children. The Bible says there is a generation that seeks God. "This is the generation of them that seek him, that seek thy face. O Jacob. Selah" (Ps. 24:6). We have been waiting for that promise even as Abraham waited. Sarah couldn't wait, so Hagar bore a child, but that was not the child of promise.

We must wait on God. We are joint heirs with Christ Jesus. We can become children of God whether we are male or female.

This all began to be revealed to me yesterday. As I prayed, I remembered the fruits of the spirit: "Love, joy, and peace, longsuffering, gentleness, goodness, faith. Meekness, temperance: against such there is no law" (Gal. 5:22–23). We can be the body of Christ. The body of Christ is His church. The body of Christ is His bride. We give gifts to a bride. Christ came to give gifts to His people.

We shall have the fruits of the Spirit. If we are to be a glorious church without spot or wrinkle, then my spirit has been reminding me about each one being his bride. Then I had a right to claim the gifts. When wisdom comes to me, I have a right to believe it is the wisdom of God, and I have a right to stand on that fact.

When the scriptures begin to reveal the mysteries of God, I have a right to believe it is the Holy Spirit. "Unto you it is given to know the mysteries of the kingdom of God" (Mark 4:11).

Jesus was tempted of the devil. "Then the devil leaves him and behold angels came and ministered unto Him" (Matt. 4:11). You never hear of the devil tormenting him anymore, in his mind. "Thou believeth that there is one God; thou does well; the devils also believe, and tremble" (James 2:19).

We can talk and encourage each other and help lift one another's loads. "Then they that feard the Lord spake often one to another: and the Lord harkened, and heard it and a book of remembrance was written before him for them that feared the Lord, and that thought upon His name" and they shall be mine, saith the Lord of host in that day when I make up my jewels; and I will spare them, as a man spared His own son that serveth him" (Mal. 3:16–17).

Someone asked me several weeks ago what the scripture means that says, "Among them that are born of women there has not risen a greater than John the Baptist: notwithstanding he that is least in the kingdom of heaven is greater than he" (Matt. 11:11). I did not know the answer. Now it is clear to me. John the Baptist preached that repentance was needed to enter the glory of the Lord in the kingdom of heaven here on earth.

If we are the least one in the kingdom of heaven, then we are greater. From the days of (John the Baptist), until now the kingdom of heaven suffers violence and the violent take it by force. That takes me to this scripture:

> "When the unclean spirit is gone out of a man, he
> walked through dry places seeking rest and finding

none. Then he saith, I will return into my house from whence I came out; and when he is comes in, he finds it empty, swept, and garnished. He goes in and takes with him seven other spirits more wicked than himself, and they enter in and dwell there: and the last state of that man is worse than the first. Even so shall it be unto this wicked generation" (Matt. 12:43–45).

Repentance is good, but it is not enough to enter the joy of the Lord. The kingdom must come; God's will must be done, on earth as it is in heaven. Jesus told the disciples, "Behold I send the promise of my Father upon you: but, tarry ye in the city of Jerusalem until ye be endued with power from on high" (Luke 24:49). That power is the Holy Spirit, who dwells in God's children.

"John bare witness of Him, and cried, saying, "This was he of whom I spake, He that cometh after me is preferred before me: for He was before me" (John 1:15). Let us receive our King. We are God's earth. We are to receive Jesus as King of kings and Lord of lords in our lives. The kingdom of God is within us. Every kingdom has a king and every king a throne; our King should be able to reign upon His throne. The King's word is final. When God speaks, His words are life; they have creating power, and they have destroying power also.

Water is wonderful. It is also terrible in a flood. Fire is comforting. Fire is also consuming. Wind is refreshing, but it is also destructive. God is a God of love and mercy and is also a God of judgment.

After reading the scripture of the unclean spirit going out of the man, I remembered the seven spirits of the churches in Revelation, how all these spirits must be cleared out of our temple before the King can sit on the throne. I know this to be true, for in the past I have been through each experience of those seven spirits.

I didn't know at the time that this was what was really happening, but now I do know. After we have overcome, that word *overcome* means a lot. Close to each admonition to hear what the Spirit is saying, we read Jesus's promise "He that hath an ear, let him hear what the spirit saith unto the churches; To him that overcometh will I give to eat of the hidden manna, and will give him a white stone, and in the stone a new name written, which no man knoweth saving he that receiveth it"(Rev. 2:7).

16

After Repentance

After we repent, we need the Spirit of truth (the Holy Spirit) to lead and guide us into all truth. "Howbeit when he the spirit of truth, is come, he will guide you into all truth: for he shall not speak of himself; but whatsoever he shall hear, that shall he speak: and he will shew you things to come" (John 16:13). A guide, doesn't always tell us beforehand what will happen, but by faith as we follow, being led by Him, He reveals the way to us. Other times, God lets us know beforehand what will happen. I remember I was so blind; I did not know that it was His Spirit comforting me.

This verse I wrote after I believed: "Listen, my child, you won't hear me say well done If you have forgotten my only son. I gave my all, precious was it not? To spread the good news, priceless was bought. I love you; I love you, rang through the night; down through the times, clearer rings today. I'm nearer my journey is not delayed. The closer I come the sweeter my voice: coaxing, and pleading come, please just one?

Can I find one who will believe I gave my all; just take one step I will not let you fall. My love will that empty place fill. To fill your life the way I want is to hear me say 'well done,' is it not?"

I would have been cut down by humankind if God had not given me His spirit. "Woe unto you, Scribes and Pharisees, hypocrites! for ye compass sea and land to make one proselyte, and when he is made, you make him twofold more the child of torment than yourselves" (Matt. 23:15). Blind leaders leading the blind. I first searched for God because of fear that was instilled in me by the preachers. That was not the way to the door of the sheepfold; it is by Jesus, and it was the love of God that sent Jesus.

I came to Jesus because of His love drawing me. I know that God's Word is the same as He is; because that is where His love drew me, through reading His Word. All the people I knew were as blind as I was. I can see that now. If people who believe would read their Bibles instead of taking someone else's opinion, then they would be led out.

The Word reads, "The kingdoms of this world have become the kingdoms of our Lord, and of His Christ; and He shall reign for ever and ever" (Rev. 11:15). I am beginning to see that the book of Revelation should be preached to every child who has believed. The whole book of Revelation is becoming alive to me personally. What is it a revelation of, if not the kingdom of God and the kingdom of heaven?

I've been thinking how the natural person is prone to keep looking for something else when he or she fails to seek what is here today. We know not the visitation of our Lord, for we are looking for it to come. Now is the day of salvation. Jesus answered. "I told you, and ye believed not: the works I do in my fathers name, they bear witness of me" (John 10:25). In Moses's day they could not enter in because of unbelief. It is no different today.

Our teachers of today have the Bible all sewed up in their minds until God's mind is to them a wrong spirit trying to enter in. "Ye do err, not knowing the scriptures, nor the power of God" (Matt. 22:29–35). I erred, not believing what I read. I was afraid I would be led wrong. The Word reads, "Ye men of Galilee, why stand ye gazing into heaven? This same Jesus, which was taken up from you into heaven, shall so come in like manner as ye have seen him go into heaven" (Acts 1:11).

Jesus says, "And then shall they see the Son of Man coming in the clouds of power and great glory" (Mark 13:26).

"The Lord cometh with ten thousand of His saints to execute judgment upon all, and to convince all that are ungodly among them of all their ungodly deeds which they have ungodly committed, and of all their hard speeches which ungodly sinners have spoken against him" (Jude 1:14–15).

17

Praise The Lord

Praise the Lord; He is bigger than the devil. He wins the battle over Lucifer. We are the temple of God the Most High. Any force that would come against that fact is Antichrist. It is against God being in our flesh.

After praying about a man who had died, I remembered the scripture: "Thou shalt worship the Lord thy God with all thy heart, and with all thy soul, and with all thy strength, and with all thy mind: and thy neighbor as thyself" (Luke 10:27). It is not just our hearts, souls, and strength but our minds also. Our minds are against God. They are death, and God is life.

Satan tried to tempt Jesus in His mind. Jesus was an overcomer. He spoke what was in His heart and mind. Satan then left Him alone. The Word works every time. King David proclaimed: "Thy word have I hid in my heart, that I might not sin against thee" (Ps. 119:11).

My God lives during our torment. My God lives. There is no hope in anyone or anything except our God—the God of heaven and the God of earth; the God who never lost a battle when His people listened to His voice. Oh, how Lucifer would like to keep the scales over our eyes, but they are going to fall off. It is the spirit that makes His words come to life; we have power over the enemy because Jesus died and arose again over death, torment, and the grave.

There is rest in the holy hill of the Lord. There is honey in the rock, and that rock is Jesus.

Oh, the love that God has for us! I believe His plan now depends on His people. "For I know the thoughts that I think towards you, saith the Lord, thoughts of peace, and not of evil, to give you an expected end. Then shall ye call upon me, and ye shall go and pray unto me, and I will heaeken unto you" (Jer. 29:11–14).

I'm not going to draw back. God has been real to me, more real than anyone in flesh and blood has been. If I can do God's will, then I will not have lived in vain. I don't know what I would do if I had any bad sickness or disease. Someone might have to comfort me day and night. I don't know, but I know that God would make a way, for I can't find a time when God ever let anyone down who put their trust in His mercy. His mercy is from everlasting to everlasting.

"This is the rest wherewith ye shall cause the weary to rest; and this is the refreshing: yet they would not hear." (Isa. 28:12). I believe God would have us trust him as a little child.

The scripture reads, "And be not conformed to this world: but be ye transformed by the renewing of your mind, that ye may prove what is that good, and accsptable, and perfect, will of God" (Rom. 12:2). We have power over the enemy of our souls, of our minds, and of our bodies. We are God's people. We are not to think it robbery to be children of God. God loves His people. No one ever cared for me like my Savior. He has won my love, and I find no fault in Him.

18

Unsearchable Riches of His Glory

The unsearchable riches of His glory are being revealed in God's Son, Christ Jesus, the only one worthy to open the book of life. Jesus Christ crucified is still the answer today and is the one and only answer as far as God is concerned. He gave His Son that we might have life and have it more abundantly. All the other offerings and sacrifices were just a shadow of things to come. They could not bring us into the garden of Eden experience: walking and talking with our God.

Jesus is our mediator; our salvation is not in any way connected to any human constitution. Jesus comes that we might be a new creation. Nothing and nobody can lift that load of guilt but Jesus. As truly as Jesus lived and died, that load of guilt is lifted.

When we confess our sin of not believing He is in us, He is just to forgive us of our sins. We are no longer in darkness.

I want to be led by God more than anything else that I know of, and I don't want it for myself, but I want it for whosoever will. "And he said it unto me, It is done. I am Alpha and Omega, the beginning and the end. I will give unto him that is athirst of the fountain of the water freely" (Rev. 21:6).

God's ways are so different from our ways that, if we don't deed our minds over to Him, we will never be able to be led any further.

His Word began to explain to me about tithes and offerings. He showed me how He wants *us*, the best of us, all of us: our hearts, souls, minds, and strength—how we are to be the first fruits. "Of His own will begat he us with the word of truth, that we should be a kind the first fruits of His creatures" (James 1:18). Also, "being the first fruits unto God and to the Lamb" (Rev. 14:4).

It comes right down to the fact that we answer to no one, but to God. "Sacrifice and offering and burnt offerings and offering for sin thou wouldest not, neither hadst pleasure therein; which are offered by the law. Then said, 'Lo! I come to do Thy will, O God' "He takes away the first, that He may establish the second" (Heb.10:7-9).

We are sanctified through the offering of the body of Jesus Christ once and for all. (Jesus became the first fruits.) We are the house of God; He comes with a fan in His hand to thoroughly purge our floor. If we think we still must pay 10 percent of our money to make it to heaven and to live as God would have us live; we might just as well be offering all the other sacrifices that were offered under the law.

But it is now the dispensation of grace. And it is not newly arrived; it has been here but hidden by the works of humankind. Can you see how glorious it is going to be? "For by grace are ye saved through faith; and that not of yourselves:it is the gift of God: Not of works, lest any man should boast" (Eph. 2:8–9).

I have always taken tithing as a way of life, but I did ask to be made into His image, no matter how different it might seem. I want to be open to whatever the Holy Spirit leads me into; for I learned that where He leads me, He feeds me. I have prayed giving myself as a first fruits unto God, and truly the windows of heaven have opened, and He has poured out a blessing I cannot contain. I have meat to eat, there is food in our storehouse, and we don't have to look for another. That's all God asked: "return to me and I will return unto you" (Mal. 3:7). "Thou shalt love the Lord thy God with all your heart, and with all your soul, and with all thy mind" (Matt. 22:37). We cannot feel condemned for not knowing this before. How can we know unless God reveals it to us?

"By one offering He hath perfected forever them that are

sanctified" (Heb. 10:14). Jesus was our first fruit, which only needs to be offered once. Read the whole chapter. He took away the first that He may establish the second.

"In vain they do worship me, teaching for doctrines the commandments of man" (Matt. 15:9). And I read this scripture this morning: "The prophets prophesy falsely, and the priest bear rule by their means; and my people love to have it s:

and what will you do in the end there of?" (Jer. 5:31).

Isaiah knew about the church that Jesus bought: "Ho! everyone that thirsteth, come ye to the waters, and he that hath no money; Come, ye, buy, and eat; yea, come and buy wine and milk without money and without price" (Isa. 55:1). Read down through the chapter; it is all there. We just need to learn about it.

The Word says we are zealous of good works: Jesus "Who gave himself for us, that he might redeem us from all iniquity, and purify unto himself a peculiar people, zealous of good works" (Titus 2:14).

I know God is leading me out by His Word. "As many that are led by the spirit of God, they are the sons of God" (Rom. 8:14).

I don't have a desire to draw back. Everything He gives is another stepping-stone to Jesus. Now I'm beginning to understand that I am different than the church world. We can be like others and draw back from the very thing that will set us free.

I remember my mother telling about when the Holy Spirit first began to be preached in their part of Kentucky. The most sincere and dedicated church people refused it. They were afraid of it. They did not continue to be sincere and dedicated. They stumbled and fell into a snare.

The very thing that would have added to their joy in serving God, when they didn't accept it, it became a snare to them. I could never expect God to lead me any further if I don't walk in the light He sheds on my pathway. For it is light; it is not darkness. It delivers.

The scripture lets us know:

> "Ye know ye were not redeemed with corruptible things such as silver and gold, from your vain conversation received by tradition from your father; but with the precious blood of Christ, as of a lamb without blemish and without spot" (1 Pet. 1:18–19).

I'm not seeking for something new or sensational. I just want to be led by the Masters' hand. I have no desire: to start a new church. I want the truth to be brought to my brothers and sisters.

God is not the author of confusion, but God is leading His children. As God shows light upon His word it may shake what we have always been taught. If we are willing and obedient, we shall eat the good of the land; if not, then we shall be devoured by the sword. God has never led us wrong; why should we even consider drawing back.

> "A new Commandment I give unto you. That ye love one another; as I have loved you. That ye also love one another" (John 13:34).

Even though my father didn't believe in paying tithes, he would give his last dime to someone in need. I feel that I belong to the same church my father belonged to—the one Jesus bought.

> "The time cometh and now is, when the true worshippers shall worship the Father in spirit and in truth: for the Father seeketh such to worship Him" (John 4:23).

They would take an offering for a need at church and my father would give his last dollar to that need. Then in the morning he might get a jacket out of the closet that he had not worn for a while. There might be twenty dollars in the pocket to supply our needs.

Our refusal to believe the truth doesn't make it a lie; it just makes us unbelievers. When I was seeking God about tithes, I went down and told my mother. She said that goes right along with the dream she had last night. She dreamed a little baby was being mistreated, and she wanted the baby so bad, but she didn't have the money to pay for it. Still, when she went to get it, the price was already paid, and she was so happy because she was going to love and take good care of it.

"Not by might, nor by power, but by my spirit saith the Lord of host" (Zech. 4:6). He seeks those who will worship Him in spirit and in truth. There is so much to search out. God is so good to us to clear just as much ground as we can possess at one time. The Old Testament is a shadow of the new covenant.

We are to wait on God. I believe that is what is meant in Revelation 3:10: "Because thou hast kept the word of my patience." We have but little strength, but we have enough to wait.

When anyone is studying to be a doctor, they spend many long hours, and that lasts only for a season. How much more should we take time for eternal values? If we give place to the devil, he is there.

The wrath of God was being poured out upon my family, but if I showed mercy unto them then God would show mercy. God does not wink at sin, but he does show mercy. Moses pleaded that, and I read in Numbers 14:18, "The Lord is longsuffering and of great mercy." I weighed the matter as to whether it might have been better to let God do as He said, but I began to see differently. It was as if He was leaving it in my hands. I began to ask the fire of God to be turned on me to cleanse out all wrath and everything that offended in His kingdom.

I can say, I don't know what tomorrow will bring, but I do know God will lead us if we believe. "Complete trust He offers on wings of prayer, faith, hope, deliverance, all three are there." That's part of a verse I wrote about five years ago. They are as real as the Bible; they are spirit, and they deliver.

I believe His Spirit let me know last year that He had called me to be a witness unto His people of His coming. He is coming the way they saw Him go away. His words are truth: Jesus "shall so come in like manner as ye have seen Him go into heaven" (Acts 1:11–12).

To be a witness, we must see something happen. The disciples were witnesses of Jesus's coming, and that transformed their lives. We are to be a witness of His second coming.

Jesus came in the flesh, and a second coming is by the spirit. He comes in clouds with great glory. He comes in us; to as many as received Him, to them He gave the power to become children of God.

It makes me realize it more after reading this scripture: "For by fire and by His sword will the Lord plead with all flesh; and the slaying of the Lord shall be many" (Isa. 66:16; see also verse 15). "Then shall that Wicked be revealed, whom the Lord shall consume with the spirit of his mouth; and shall destroy with the brightness of his coming" (2 Thess. 2:8). Our God is a consuming fire.

Now if God is in us, that fire is in us. Jesus walked right here on Earth, after He was resurrected. He was not the same. In the natural He lost his natural blood, yet they could see Him, and He ate as you and I. Yet He had new blood. He gave up His life. He had newness of life. I spiritually had gone through these torments. I believe many times we go through these experiences not getting out of them what God has for us, until our eyes are open; and then can we see what Jesus paid the price for us to have. We are filled with His Spirit, even as Jesus was. "Truly I am full of power by the spirit of the Lord" (Micah 3:8). We know this doesn't agree with traditions and man-made doctrines, but that is what Jesus preached.

The Scribes and Pharisees were carnal minded as some of our leaders are today. If they could not see something, then they could not believe it. But we shall never see the results of faith until we have it. If we believe Jesus is the Christ, the Son of the living God, then to us He is. He will never leave us or forsake us.

There is just one thing about it: either I am of God, and He reveals the truth, or else I am a child of the devil, and this is all false. Jesus was fed butter and honey "that He may know to refuse the evil and choose the good" (Isa. 7:15). Good things come from His heavenly Father.

God never mistreated Jesus. Therefore, He had complete trust in Him. It is not that we loved God, but that God first loved us and proved that love. That love commands trust. Satan comes only to destroy, to steal, and to kill, but Jesus comes that we might have life.

A church did not believe that you should do business on Sunday. One of the members owned a grocery store. Another member came by on Sunday and asked him to sell him some milk as his baby needed milk. He opened the store and sold him some milk for the baby.

The church members found out about him opening his store on Sunday. They turned him out of the church and took his name off their church book.

My father took up for the man who had sold the milk, and they turned my father out of the church and took my father's name off their church book also.

The next night at church one of the men stood up and told how he had smashed his little finger and how badly it hurt. He said it hurt his whole body. He then compared how turning the men out of the church had hurt the whole body of believers. He pointed out that the leaders had done wrong by turning them out of the church. Sadly, the church leaders didn't change their minds.

This was many years ago, and the leaders are deceased.

I was thinking this morning that there aren't any gloomy days of sorrow, no matter if the storms are raging. We can read the Word and know wherein we stand. "Wherefor let him that thinketh he standeth take heed lest he fall" (1 Cor. 10:12). When the Holy Spirit speaks, we can know where we stand.

Everything is going to be shaken. Sometimes it takes quite a shaking to open our blinded eyes, but God knows what is best for us (Isa. 30:32). "In battles of shaking" (Hag. 2:6). God shows us His love and it is always greater than what we have been taught. We learn to see things differently, as He shakes our thinking.

I believe the problem is our spiritual eyes; for I keep thinking of narrow-minded people. If one part of the Bible is to be taken spiritually, then I believe it all should be taken spiritually to do the work God had planned for it to do. Jesus said, "For many I say unto you, will seek to enter in, and shall not be able" (Luke 13:24). We give God everything except our mind.

Perfect love casts out fear. If we have perfect love, we will trust God unreservedly, listening to His voice and knowing He will lead us even as He led Jesus. Jesus knew that God heard Him for that happened when He prayed for Lazarus. "I know that thou heareth me always: but because of the people that stand by I said it, that they may believe that thou hast sent me" (John 11:42). We can know when God answers prayer. We may never see that person.

19

Three Greater Works

After the service Thursday night, I asked the Holy Spirit what the three greater works were that He had done that night. The Holy Spirit said to move mountains, shake minds, and heal loads.

First, there is a natural before there is a spiritual. The serpent was in the garden of Eden with God as He walked and talked with man. God created the serpent. Then he was revealed when he deceived Adam and Eve. They had a choice to obey God or not to obey Him.

In the spiritual realm, Satan, that old serpent, is in our spiritual realm. He has not been revealed as such. He has deceived the people down through the ages, but his time is at an end when he is revealed.

I have often wondered why Jesus taught His disciples to pray, "Lead us not into temptation." I could not see how He could ever be leading us into the path of the devil. But now it is clear. He allowed the children in the wilderness to be tempted to see if they would call upon Him. Instead they murmured and complained and did not serve God. "All power is of God" (Rom. 13:1). He is allowing Satan to reign to try the people to see if they will cry and repent so that He will hear them and heal the land. But instead they love darkness rather than light. The Lord is "not willing that any should perish but all should come to repentance" (2 Peter 3:9). God has set before you this day "life and good, and death and evil" (Deut. 30:15–18). If we choose good, we shall have life; if we choose evil, we shall have death.

We don't always let the Spirit lead us, and then we can be tempted.

I read in the Word that all power is going to be shaken in heaven (Isa. 13:13; Hag 2:6–7; Matt. 24:29; Mark 13:25; Luke 21:26; Heb. 12:26). That wicked one shall be revealed. (2 Thes. 2:10) Because they received not the love of the truth, that they might be saved."

There is no power but that which is ordained of God. God caused Pharaoh's heart to be hardened that He might show His power to the children of Israel by leading them out of bondage. Pharoah would not have had power, if God had not permitted it. "I am the first, and I am the last; and beside me there is no God" (Isa. 44:6). There is going to be a tried-and-true people: those who have chosen to serve Him and to have no other gods before Him, a people who, when they are tempted, will submit themselves to God and resist the devil. A people whose garments are washed in the blood of the Lamb.

In Luke 10:18, we read that Jesus said, "I saw Satan fall from heaven as lightning." Jesus said He was with His Father from the beginning. Should He not have also seen the end of Satan? Through the name of Jesus, the devil would have to bow. Jesus paid the price that we might have life. "When ye shall see Jerusalem compassed about with armies know that the desolation thereof is nigh" (Luke 21:20). "Behold, I come quickly; hold that fast which thou hast, that no man take thy crown" (Rev. 3:11).

Paul says, "God is faithful who will not suffer you to be tempted above that ye are able; but with the temptation also make a way to escape, that ye may be able to bear it" (1 Cor. 10:13).

"That the trial of your faith, being that much more precious than of gold that perished, though it be tried with fire, might be found unto praise and honour and glory at the appearing of Jesus Christ" (1 Pet. 1:7).

I heard my pastor say one night: that the devil wasn't sending anyone to his burning dungeon. I never heard it that way, but that began to set me free. God is in the driver's seat. We are to fear God, not the devil.

Satan could not touch Job unless God permitted him to. Job was the man God said he was. Job was greater in the end, than in the beginning. In Job 2:1, we read, "Satan came also among them to present himself before the Lord." Is he not in the heavenly realms; this day making out that he is God? And in Daniel 11:45–12:1:

> "He shall plant the tabernacle of his palace between the seas in the glorious holy mountain; yet he shall come to his end, and none shall help him. At that time shall Michael stand up, the great prince which standeth for the children of thy people: and there shall be a time of trouble, such as never was since there was a nation even to that same time: and at that time thy people shall be delivered, everyone that shall be written in the book."

> "The Lord will redeem the soul of his servants: and none of them that trust in him shall be desolate" (Ps. 34:22).

If I have erred in spirit. I pray God would show me. I know myself; I cannot understand the Word of God. My desire is to have the mind of Christ.

20

To Open the Blind Eyes

My insides have cried for days, "Open the blinded eyes, restore sight to the blind; I will give you sight for the blind. I would see even as He sees. I would stand even as He stands and that His people would see even as He sees."

Paul wrote that he had not apprehended; he could see more. "I press toward the mark for the prize of the high calling of God in Christ Jesus" (Phil. 3:12–14).

"I will come to visions and revelations of the Lord" (2 Cor. 12:1–5).

"To whom God would make known, what is the riches of the glory of this mystery among the Gentiles: which is Christ in you the hope of glory" (Col. 1:27).

Why do you look for another? Why do we look forward to that life after this robe of flesh dies more than we look forward to life right here and now? Jesus came that we might have life and have it more abundantly. Oh, I thank God for life—real life, in Christ Jesus. There is a new heaven and a new earth. We cannot know spiritual death; we cannot know spiritual sorrow; and we cannot know spiritual pain, for all things are passed.

God is a spirit; we must worship Him in spirit and truth. His spirit bears witness with our spirits that we are the children of God. "The dead in Christ shall rise first" (1 Thess. 4:16). That ties in with

Revelation: if we are dead in Christ, then it is no more I that live, but Christ in me. We are not of this world; we will sit in heavenly (peaceful) places. The struggles of this life have ended. We know in whom we have believed for if His love is perfected in us, we will not know fear. And if we don't know fear, then we won't have torment. We are serving the God who was before the beginning. He is the beginning. He is the ending—the same yesterday, today, and forever. He changes not.

> "As it is appointed unto men once to die, but after this the judgement" (Heb. 9:27).

> "For if we would judge ourselves, we should not be judged" (1 Cor. 11:31).

We have to say goodbye completely to our minds. If Adam and Eve had said goodbye to their minds, they could have stayed in the garden. We still have that choice. I believe our minds constantly breed contempt: "The imagination of the thoughts of his heart was only evil continually" (Gen. 6:5).

The faith that God gives us cannot be taken away by people, for it was not given by them; so they cannot touch it. In the Word we read that. "Knowing this first, no prophecy of the scripture is of any private interpretation" (2 Pet. 1:20).

Believe that no matter where we are in God, the scriptures can bring life unto us. One example I remember is how it reads, "Consider the lilies of the field, how they grow: they toil not, neither do they spin" (Matt. 6:28–29). How much more would He clothe us! When we first come to Christ, that scripture is a comfort, reassuring us that He is that mindful of us. Then as we walk on, we find that He will never leave us or forsake us. Then as we walk on, we find He will clothe us with righteousness, peace, and joy, with wisdom and knowledge, and with the garments of salvation and the perfection of beauty.

The scriptures: are life to young and old; poor and rich, sin-sick and redeemed. They are a store house of living life. When the Word is applied, it works. It does not know failure. His Word is the same as He is. When we come to God, we must believe that God is. Then as we walk on, we learn to know that He is God. Not one of His promises has ever failed. "But ye, brethren, are not in darkness, that that day should overtake you as a thief. Ye are all the children of light, and the children of the day: we are not of the night, nor of darkness" (1 Thess. 5:4).

Jesus has said, "Heaven and earth shall pass away, but my words shall not pass away" (Matt. 24:35).

This morning the phrase "for perpetual generations" stood out in Genesis 9:12. The dictionary defined it as lasting forever or continuing or constant.

Our lives are like vapor. If we could really grasp the meaning of that we would truly redeem the time. Maybe when we die there won't be anyone to help God's people, but if we can proclaim the truth while we are here, then the truth will stand when we are long forgotten. That brought back to my mind how the saints that have passed on have influenced our lives. No matter how long we live, it is still a short time.

Only what is founded on Jesus will stand—not our ideas, not what seems to be right, not traditions, not enticing words of human wisdom. Only the truth will deliver and stand. The rock that has withstood the ages is Jesus. I believe He stands taller and straighter than ever before and shines brighter and brighter unto the perfect day. If someone had told me these things twenty years ago, I would have said that person was completely wrong. A carnal mind cannot comprehend the things of God. When we find our minds are our worst enemies, we will begin to awaken out of sleep.

I believe this will take us all the way. When God moves, we move. There can be nothing but victory; He never lost a battle, so we can stay on the winning side.

Oh, hallelujah! Only God knows the peace of heart, soul, mind, and body that we can have. It's peace such as I have never known before.

I believe my mind will completely have peace before long.

My spirit is teaching me about leading low lives. Once I wrote: "Lead lowly lives now, and when your children are old, they won't depart from it."

"Let nothing be done through strife or vain glory; but in lowliness of mind let each esteem other better than themselves" (Phil. 2:3). He wants a humble people that will lean not to their own understanding—not only our hearts and souls humbled but our minds as well. If we sit at His feet with stout hearts and cluttered minds, then we can't receive what our souls cry out for. If we are to be led, then we must be willing. It is not a narrow-minded way. There is no boundary to the mind of Christ; all things are His in heaven and earth. He will not withhold anything good from us if we walk uprightly.

"Then if any man shall say, unto you, Lo, here is Christ, or there; believe it not. For there shall arise false Christ, and false prophets, and shall show great signs and wonders; in as much as if it were possible, they shall deceive the very elect." (Matt. 24:23). He said every eye shall behold him. We know when Jesus comes and sits on His throne. No one will tell us but the angels. For days I could hear the angels singing "Holy, Holy Night"; then months went on and I could hear them singing, "Joy to the World." Then I could hear them singing, "Glory to the newborn King." Then when trials would come, they were singing to me "Mercy on the newborn King." Then when the trial was over, they rejoiced again: "Holy, Holy, Holy," the angels sang. Then there were times when I needed it most, but "I find no fault in Him." The Comforter is truly a comfort.

I remember one time; last winter I felt so bound I cried, "Give me liberty or give me death!" If we lean upon our own understanding, we fall flat on our faces. So, when we finally realize our ways are not His ways, then we put our understanding in the background. It is by faith that we obtain forgiveness for the sin of not believing that He is in us. So, it is by faith all the way. If we begin in the spirit surely, we can end in the spirit.

"Israel shall be saved in the Lord with an everlasting salvation: ye shall not be ashamed nor confounded, world without end. (Isa. 45:17)

"For the Lord will help me; therefore, shall I not be confounded: therefore, have I set my face like a flint, and I know that I shall not be ashamed. (Isa. 50:7)"

We have an up-to-date God and loving Father whose portion is His children.

"I John saw the Holy city, the new Jerusalem, coming down from God out of heaven, prepared like a bride adorned for her husband" (Rev. 21:2). I believe all that heaven affords can be ours.

I don't believe the resurrection from the dead, that Paul talked at that time about attaining was the resurrection of his earthly body—although God is all-powerful, and it could mean just that. What makes me believe that, is that right after I believed, every time I would pray, that would come out of my mouth, "That I may know Him in the power of His resurrection" (Phil. 3:10). When spiritual life began to come I didn't pray that. We know that we have passed from death unto life. When they asked Jesus about the resurrection, he told them, "They which shall be accounted worthy to obtain that world, and the resurrection from the dead, neither marry nor given in marriage: neither can they die anymore for they are equal unto the angels; and are the children of God the children of the resurrection" (Luke 20:35-36).

One day I was pondering this over, and in Matthew 22:29–32, Jesus told those who deny the resurrection that they were wrong, "Ye do err, not knowing the scriptures or the power of God."

"Paul said, I protest by your rejoicing which I have in Christ Jesus our Lord, I die daily" (Matt. 22:29). He believed in a resurrection for as he died daily, he was resurrected daily. I believe we can attain to all the fullness of God by His Son, Christ Jesus. We have always been scared to death at hearing preachers preach about tormenting fire, how this world is going to be burned up.

Our God is a consuming fire. The fire of His love purges, refines, and cleanses. We can't bring things back to our memory. "Whom the Lord shall consume with the spirit of his mouth" (2 Thess. 2:8). God made a covenant with Noah that he would never again smite everything living as he had done. The fire of the Holy Spirit consumes the old heaven and the old earth. I know it sounds as if I am out on a limb. Jesus is the only one worthy to open the Lamb's book of life.

My pastor said that if we stayed meek and humble, we would never be deceived. "For I am meek and lowly in heart, and ye shall find rest unto your soul" (Matt. 11:29). We must go all the way; there is no stopping off. It is all spiritual for God is a spirit. Worshipping must be in the spirit. Jesus had perfect fellowship with God the Father while here on this earth, and we are joint heirs who by faith can inherit all things. "Let him which is on the housetop not to come down to take anything out of his house" (Matt. 24:17). There is a way that seems right; then there is a way that *is* right. If we are on the housetop, let us stay there, and proclaim it, and don't come down.

We will stay up there, for where God leads us, He will feed us. We have not left anything in this house to come down after. Jesus never retreated, but the devil did.

God is so good. He is such a merciful God that He is mindful of us, far beyond our understanding. He is more real than you and I are real. When all the shackles are shaken off, then there can be some manifestation of the children of God. Oh, just think of our minds being completely free!—and know of a surety that they will be. The love God has for His children shall not fail us. When we are wrong, He shows us we are wrong. He doesn't allow us to stumble around until we fall, if we submit ourselves unto Him.

21

Mercy, Mercy from Our God

Mercy, mercy, mercy from our God. He will have mercy, for He comes to have love and mercy for His people. Oh, the mercy of God! It is truly overwhelming. Shouting and dancing and singing are all a means of deliverance, but all the while the mercy of God is what is holding us close in His bosom. "Fear thou not; for I am with thee: be not dismayed; for I am thy God: I will strengthen thee; yea, I will help thee; yea, I will uphold thee with the right hand of my righteousness" (Isa. 41:10). It seems I have never been able to go along with the crowd, and sometimes it is just Jesus and me, but He never failed to feed where He leads.

When I first believed, I asked the Holy Spirit to show me what He was really like. I believed that tradition would be the greatest obstacle standing in my way. As I heard nothing about the love of God. Do this and do that and God would love me and accept me. Was the preaching I heard. I was full of how to worship God by the way the ministers taught. (Col. 2:8)." Beware lest any man spoil you through philosophy and vain deceit, after the tradition of men, after the rudiments of the world, and not after Christ. I knew nothing about His love. It was not by spirit and truth, but the glorious part of it all is that He never condemned me. No matter how blind I was, He never pointed a finger at me. Little by little He led me step-by-step. He let me walk, loving me and comforting me all the way. I thought I was right, how I was serving Him, but I was as blind as the Sadducees and Pharisees. I honestly was working my way to be holy. I was cleaning up the outside of the platter, but Jesus was cleaning the inside, getting rid of my fears, doubts, and unbelief. Oh, the mercy of our God! I thought I had the answers; I thought I was doing what was pleasing in His sight. I didn't believe that His Spirit was in me, and that spirit is love.

We are to follow that Spirit, which will lead us into all truth. If I had believed, I would not have had to go through all those outward motions. It was like fasting to see if God would hear me. God will hear me and accept me. I did all this in my own power, trying to please God, when all the time it was unbelief. If I had believed that God was within me, I would not have been trying to get good enough for Him.

22

God Loves His People

God loves His people. He's not willing that any perish. There is a way that seems right but isn't always the right way. Only God's way and only His Word will stand. Oh, how God loves His people! He stands with open arms while we turn this way and that way, doing everything except resting in His care. It's only the truth that will set us free. If we don't pray until we receive the truth, then we will never be set free. It is always good to remember that God is the potter, and we are the clay. He has power to break us to make us more beautiful, whenever we don't shape up the way He had planned.

Aren't we glad He has that power? The only way we will ever be able to please Him is to keep quoting that scripture: "Not my will, but thine be done" (Luke 22:42).

I was praying this morning, and Jeremiah 6:16 came to me: "Ask for the old path where in is the good way" was the portion that I remembered.

I remembered how, when I was a child at home, my mother and father used to trust the Lord for healing. This one time I was about five years old; and one of my older brothers, Arvie, had an attack of appendicitis, and for two weeks he lay swollen and groaning in pain. I cried, and prayed, as I knelt by my little chair. The church people came and prayed. Still, he was the same.

Then one night they all came again. Everyone cried like a funeral and the minister quoted the scripture: "This sickness is not unto death, but for the glory of God, that the Son of God might be glorified thereby" (John 11:4). He wasn't healed that night, and my uncle told my father that if he let that boy lie there and die, he would have the law down on him. My grandmother, who was a Christian, gave my mother money to help on the funeral expenses before she went back to Kentucky. Where we lived, we could see the cemetery from our house and that haunted us.

Dad told Mom for them both to search themselves before God so they could stand on God's Word. A few days after the minister spoke about the sickness, the minister was on his way back to our house, and he was talking to the Lord, and he asked God to have Arvie be healed when he got there. Sure enough, all at once Arvie quit having pain, got up and ate, and started playing and pulling his little wagon. Mom and Dad said after that scripture was spoken, nothing could shake their faith. My dad said when things began to look dark, "God may have to take our little boy, but I'm going to trust Him, that He knows best." That goes along with the scripture in Job 13:15, which says, "Though He slay me yet will I trust Him." That is not the only time God healed in our home. My parents knew what God could do, and they waited on Him.

Doctors are used by God to help heal His children, also. Thank God for doctors.

My dad could have taken my brother to the hospital, and he likely would have been operated on and recovered. That would not have been finding out what God has for His children.

One time a Christian friend had a large sore just above her knee. The doctor had told her it was bone cancer. One morning she felt God prompted her to go and see my mother and father. "Oh Lord how great are your works! And thy thoughts are very deep" (Ps. 92:5). She arrived, and the spirit of weeping came upon them; "Jesus wept" (John 11:33–35). Then they prayed, and while they prayed, the skin grew over that place in her knee. Then the spirit of rejoicing came, and they rejoiced in the spirit.

She was so happy; she went to where her husband worked and showed him what God had done. Trusting God was against most people's way of thinking. Salvation is also. To have that load of guilt erased is the greatest miracle of all; to have our bodies healed must be a desire of God's. For the Word says, "I wish above all things, that thou mayest prosper and be in health, even as thy soul prospereth." (3 John 1:2).

We know God is going to have a people who trust Him. We know that, and if we think we are going to be that people and still not trust Him, then we need to shake our thinking until we see Jesus, for when we see Him, we shall know that He is life.

Our bodies are included in this verse: "Heart, soul, mind and strength [i.e., body]" (Luke 10:27). When our souls were searching for God, we prayed until deliverance came. When our hearts were heavy laden, we prayed and waited until His Spirit came. When our minds were confused and tormented and there seemed to be no way out, we prayed for months and years until help came. When our bodies were sick, our God cared about that too.

I know God uses doctors to heal His children, for not all may believe.

"Heaven and earth shall pass away, but my words shall not pass away" (Matt. 24:35). He wants a people who will stand on His Word. When a member of the church died and I walked out of that room, I remembered those same words. "Heaven and earth shall pass away, but my words shall not pass away." The only way we can believe in salvation is to stand on His Word. ("'Tis so sweet to trust in Jesus, just to take Him at His word," to quote the hymn by Louisa M.R. Stead; the verse of that song just came to me).

God doesn't change, but people do. When Moses was leading God's people; if they didn't move when God said to move, then they were in darkness.

In the Word, Jesus told us,

> "Many will say to me in that day, Lord, Lord have we not prophesied in thy name? and in thy name have cast out devils? And in thy name done many wonderful works? Then I will profess unto them, I never knew you: depart from me, ye that work iniquity" (Matt. 7:22–23).

> "Let us hold fast the profession of our faith without wavering; (for He is faithful that promised;) And let us consider one another to provoke unto love and to good works:" (Heb. 10:23–24).

"Thinking is a word, not much used today. Thinking will bring you back when you start to stray. Thinking can bring fear or peace of mind; upon what we think makes a difference we will find." That is a portion of a poem that I wrote several years ago.

King David let us know " Thy word have I hidden in mine heart, that I might not sin against thee" (Ps. 119:11). If we are not standing on God's Word, that is not of faith, and that which is not of faith will let us down. Our God has never failed anyone who trusted in Him. God is so good.

He is in all things that happen to us. We can see Him in every circumstance. That is exactly where I found Him. In His word. God doesn't expect as much out of us as we expect out of ourselves for He is love, and love wants the best for us.

God sure has been merciful to me. I was naked and blind, yet He loved me and comforted and called me His love. Many times, He has told me He would heal His love. Little did I realize His love in me needed healing, so it could shine forth! Like this Donna Fargo song, they play on the radio now:

YOU CAN'T BE A BEACON IF YOUR LIGHT DON'T SHINE

"There is a little light in us by God's design."

23

Holy Is the God of Abraham

Holy is the God of Abraham, Isaac, and Jacob, and holy is our God. A holy nation under God is indivisible, with liberty and justice for all. Several weeks ago, I read about God taking a nation from within a nation: "take Him a nation from the midst of another nation" (Deut. 4:34).

Step-by-step He leads us out if we will keep our hearts wide open before Him. He tries the reins of our hearts. Where our treasures are, there will our hearts be also. It has been hard to get the mind of humankind out of God's mind for I was brought up under humankind's mind. I guess my soul was sold into bondage. If we can find favor with the King, that is what counts. I believe if our heart is set on things above, God will lead us out of our minds, for in this world we shall have tribulation. The work that God would have us do is not of this world, for our ways are not God's ways.

I turned back to Isaiah 58:13–14. The Sabbath day, or the holy day of the Lord, seems to be charity or perfect love, when we love God with all our hearts, souls, minds, and bodies, and our neighbors as ourselves. Verse 13 reads, "not doing my own ways, nor finding my pleasures, or speaking mine own words." Also,

(Mark 12:30) "Thou shall love the Lord thy God with all thy

heart, and with all thy soul, and with all thy mind, and with all thy strength: this is the first commandment."

Then the King sits on His throne in His holy temple. Let all the earth be silent. If we by the spirit mortify the deeds of the body, we shall live. More and more I'm seeing that "He has shewed thee, O man, what is good: and what doth the Lord require of thee, but to do justly, and to love mercy, and to walk humbly with thy God" (Mic. 6:8). "In quietness and confidence shall be our strength." (Isa. 30:15).

If any person speaks, let it be as an oracle of God. If we speak, it should edify the body of Christ; it should be uplifting, upbuilding.

Someone called me and talked on and on about church. When she hung up, I remembered the scripture that mentions "wells without water" (2 Peter 2:17). My faith was not built up; the words that she said did not edify. Now, that person doesn't come very often, but I know God still loves her. It is indeed a narrow way, and few there be that find it. God did not let me know that to find fault with her but to keep from getting caught in the same snare. Not everyone who says, "Lord, Lord" will enter in, "but he that doth the will of Father which is in haven" (Matt. 7:21).

"Ye are our epistle written in our hearts, known and read of all men" (2 Cor. 3:2). People are reading our lives. God's Word writes upon our hearts and minds by the spirit, and the lives we live reflect what is in our hearts and minds. We must not bear false witness. "Let every one that names the name of Christ depart from iniquity" (2 Tim. 2:19).

A lady at a church was telling how her husband had been let down so many times by professing Christians that it was hard for him to have confidence. I believe God wants to raise him up, with many more who have been trodden upon. The truth will be brought to everyone. Some will awaken to life everlasting; others will turn away unto shame and everlasting contempt.

I was talking to a minister who told me about a man who had killed himself in a motel room over the weekend. This man had come to him to talk over his troubles, but the minister never could seem to help him. He said it was like a block that he couldn't get through to him. The night he shot himself he had called the minister's home and didn't get to talk to him, as he was in a church service. He said he couldn't be in two places at one time.

I told him how my daughter had woken up just the night before and couldn't go back to sleep for worrying about a cat that was run over in front of our house; while she was waiting for the school bus. The cat had stayed with her cat, and she was fond of it. She called me into her room, and I prayed for her and began to call that mind out of her mind, and within minutes she was asleep. I told him I could have tried to explain to her and begged her to forget about it, but she still would have stayed awake. But when we prayed, God took that out of her mind.

I did not fully see then why I was telling him that. Now I see why, as I am writing this. Our thinking cannot deliver minds; only the Spirit of God can, and this minister needed to know why he couldn't help that man. It seemed to thrill his soul as we talked. He couldn't understand how the scriptures were so clear to me. I told him about when I had gotten down on the floor on my knees with the Bible and asked God to show me what He was really like. How I had hungered and thirsted and how God was satisfying me. He asked what church I belonged to, and I told him the church of the living God, the one Paul talked about. Real satisfaction comes when we obey, giving of ourselves, showing others the way. I'm finding out God's love doesn't fail.

The pure of heart shall see God. A friend of mine says the congregation at a church she attends is complaining about how the pastor talks to them. Her God will bring her out and then into a sheepfold, to where there is a good shepherd and not a hireling (John 10:12–14). He is driving more away than he is bringing in. You can't beat the sheep and get them to follow; you must lead them. Sometimes you may even have to carry them.

"Holy perfection" just came to my mind. There must be a

perfection that is unholy. "Be ye perfect, even as your Father in heaven is perfect" (Matt. 5:48).

Just as there are miracles and holy miracles; God's love is a big love: it covers the whole world.

I know we should pray for the leaders of our country. "I exhort therefore, that, first of all, supplications, prayers and giving of thanks, be made for all men, for Kings, and for all that are in authority; that we may lead a quiet and peaceable life in all godliness and honesty" (1 Tim. 2:1–2). They have great and terrible forces that they can control. They have a choice to make whether to use them for good or for destruction. When we pray, God can change their minds, and they won't even know why they do as they do.

I believe charity is holy love, as it doesn't fail. "For all the promises of God in Him are yea, and in him Amen, unto the glory of God by us." (2 Cor. 1:20).

Since God raised my mind, I believe there isn't anything impossible for Him. God had loved me when I was wrong about things. Now I can love and comfort others, knowing that God is faithful and not slack concerning His promises. There is no law against love. It does cover a multitude of sins. There shall be peace on earth, for those to whom Jesus speaks peace.

The Bible says, "When He putteth forth His own sheep, he goes before them, and the sheep follow Him: for they know his voice" (John 10:4). If we are first partakers of our first fruits, then we know they will work for someone else. As I was praying yesterday, I felt impressed that the Holy Spirit was showing me that He wants His children to live to love Him. If we love God with the same love that He has for us, then we won't fail Him.

We need to build on the solid rock, which is Christ Jesus, the chief cornerstone that the builders rejected. There will not be left one stone on top of another for when the stones are shaken, the untempered mortar will crumble and fall. "And her prophets have daubed them with untempered mortar, seeing vanity and, divining lies unto them. Saying, Thus, saith the Lord thy God, when the Lord hath not spoken"

(Ezek. 22:28). Traditions and humankind's ideas will separate us from our God and from walking and talking with Him.

Jesus could see the end from the beginning. It is recorded that "Looking unto Jesus the author and finisher of our faith; who for the joy that was set before Him endured the cross, despising the shame, and is set down at the right hand of the throne of God" (Heb. 12:2).

Sometimes our load becomes great, but His yoke is easy, and His burden is light. Jesus is that friend who is always standing there. "He saith to Moses, I will have mercy on whom I will have mercy, and I will have compassion on whom I will have compassion" (Rom. 9:15). God is so good to His people, a people who are helpless and hopeless without His help. It is surely wonderful how gently He leads us; step-by-step, He knows just where we are. Every time I read the Bible, I find something I have never seen before.

I never could understand why the devil has to be amid God's people when we come together. He needs to be there so the truth can prevail over falsehood. For everything is brought to light.

I believe we are to be the little duck in a big puddle. All that is required of us is to be willing vessels full of God's love, more willing to give than to receive. God seems to make it so plain how we bear the marks of Jesus in our own bodies; the spirits that come against us don't see us. They are fighting against the God within us. That will always be true; they will continue to come against us, but we can ride on top of the waters instead of drowning under the attack. We had better heap on the armor for the battle is raging.

The Bible is another book altogether different than what we thought it was after God begins to reveal it by the Spirit. Although Jesus told all those parables, He was not casting His pearls before swine, because they couldn't even comprehend the meaning of what He was talking about. "To whom much is given much is required" (Luke 12:48). Jesus said, "It is easier for a camel to go through the eye of the needle than for a rich man to enter into the kingdom of God" (Matt. 19:24).

Righteousness, peace, and joy. We can have the wisdom of God, but until we learn to freely give as we have freely received, we cannot know the peace of God. The rich man did not realize God had given him his riches. It really becomes a snare unto us: we know to do well, but we don't do it. I realize more and more that the greatest sermon we will ever preach is the life we live. Was Jesus lifted? If He wasn't, then all was in vain.

I have learned to know a God of love and mercy. It is holy mercy, mercy where humankind would never have had mercy, a mercy unlimited, a mercy that will shake you. It is unspeakably long-suffering, not willing that any should perish. It can all be told in one word: *love*, for God is love. If everything is done in love, then God is lifted.

I began to see how faultfinding brings judgment upon us. "Judge not" (Matt. 7:1). I was wondering why some people never seem to keep their heads above water. I began to see it was because of the harsh judgment they give out with no mercy. When it comes back to them, they fall under the load. When we find fault, that leaves us wide open for Satan to put a load upon us that is not of God. The loads that Satan puts upon us are too heavy to bear. Jesus said, "For my yoke is easy and my burden is light" (Matt. 11:30). When we carry a holy load, our minds aren't tormented. We have complete trust in God. We can attain that love God longs for us to have, by His grace.

A carnal mind cannot begin to comprehend His love. His love covers a multitude of sins; it is as if it never was there. Such love is unknown on the human level. The kingdom of God is peaceful and beautiful, and it is within us. The kingdom of God is a house ruled by God's love. We are to be that house when all the earth keeps silence. We are not a little island; we are not to hide it under a bushel.

The Antichrist spirit is set against that kingdom: "Every spirit that confesses not that Jesus Christ is come in the flesh is not of God: and this is that spirit of antichrist, whereof ye have heard that it should come; and even now is already in the world" (1 John 4:3–5). "Ye are of God, little children, and have overcme them: because greater is he that is within you, than he that is in the world." God is going to win out but not until He can receive all the glory for He is the King of glory. The battle is the Lord's, the victory is His, and the glory is His.

I realize that until all of self is put down, the glory that belongs to God will be blemished. When He is high and lifted, then shall all people come unto Him. "They shall not teach every man his neighbour, and every man his brother, saying, Know the Lord: for all shall know me, from the least to the greatest" (Heb. 8:11).

"By this shall all men know that ye are my disciples, if you have love one to another" (John 13:35).

I wrote a verse about how there are two kinds of people: mine and thine. That kind of shook me up. Here I thought I was His kind; then months later He began to show me His love that He would have dwell within us. He is indeed a true shepherd and not a hireling for He has written His Word on our hearts and minds. "When the enemy shall come in like a flood, the spirit of the Lord shall lift up a standard against him" (Isa. 59:19).

He is such a good, kind, and gentle teacher, ever leading us into what is best for us to bring out the Holy Spirit in us. He has showed me how there is never any reason to dispute the scriptures if Jesus is lifted; for wherever we are in Christ, the scriptures are life unto us and can have an entirely different meaning to each one of us. We are the ones who set the boundaries in our own minds for with God all things are possible. The scripture that says, "Offend not your brother because of meat" is indeed spiritual (1 Cor. 8:13).

"Hast thou faith? Have it to thyself before God" (Rom. 14:22). My prayer is that I might be a willing vessel filled with God's love that I may be able to impart that love to someone else. As we mature, we can impart and show forth the true Father. We will always have opposition, but if we are rooted and grounded in His love, we shall not be shaken.

"Heaven and earth shall pass away, but my word shall not pass away" (Matt. 24:35). I truly thank God for the Word that He writes upon our hearts and minds.

His Word is, indeed, the Gospel of Peace.

Printed in the United States
By Bookmasters